HEAVENLY HUMOR

for the

Cat Lover's Soul

HEAVENLY HUMOR

for the

Cat Lover's Soul

75 Fur-Filled
Inspirational Readings
from Fellow Feline Fans

BARBOUR
PUBLISHING

Our mission is to publish and distribute inspirational products offering exceptional value and biblical encouragement to the masses.

Member of the
Evangelical Christian
Publishers Association

Contents

SECTION 4—THE CAT'S MEOW: LOVE

SECTION 5—CURIOSITY KILLED THE CAT: TRUSTING GOD

SECTION 10—THE CAT WHO SWALLOWED THE CANARY:
OBEDIENCE

WHEN IT RAINS CATS (AND DOGS!): GOD'S PROTECTION

Protect specially, dear Lord,
The little cat who is the companion of our home,
Keep her safe as she goes abroad,
And bring her back to comfort us.

AN OLD RUSSIAN PRAYER

FACING THE GIANTS

ANNA M. AQUINO

Then David said to the Philistine, "You come to me with a sword, a spear, and a javelin, but I come to you in the name of the LORD of hosts, the God of the armies of Israel, whom you have taunted. This day the LORD will deliver you up into my hands, and I will strike you."

1 SAMUEL 17:45–46 NASB

While I was growing up, we had a cat named Lynx. He looked like a long-haired gray lynx bobcat. He had a regal way about him. Though we had three other cats and a dog, it was well known that Lynx ruled the "animal kingdom" in our home.

I remember one day in particular when my aunt brought her two dogs over for a visit. Her dogs were enormous Great Danes that reminded me of miniature horses. All of our animals—including our dog—found a place to hide, but not Lynx. He stood in the middle of the living room, puffed his chest out, then planted his feet and sat down. You could imagine the thoughts going through Lynx's head. He was declaring his authority. Every time one of the

Great Danes had the audacity to walk by him, Lynx balled up his paw and swatted at the intruding beast. A "little" gray cat fighting off these enormous dogs was comical. Lynx didn't even come up to their knees, but he declared ownership of his space. Eventually the dogs avoided Lynx altogether.

This tale is a great reminder of the story of David and Goliath. I'm sure watching David and Goliath fight was very similar. I wonder if David even came up to Goliath's knees. I'm sure the soldiers watched in both horror and amusement thinking that there was no way David could take Goliath down. But David's size didn't matter. All that mattered was what God said. David knew that one day he would be king, and he knew that God's authority and power was greater than that of any giant. David was able to boldly walk out onto that field and declare that the Philistine would be defeated that day, because he knew God was on his side.

We all have walked through similar situations. The enemies in our life seem to tower over us. We can look at these situations and view them as "Goliaths." We can look at the giant and want to run. Or we can move forward in faith, knowing that God is bigger than any giant in our lives. We can be confident knowing that if God is for us, then who can be against us? Approach life's giants with boldness, knowing that you are a child of the King of kings and Lord of lords!

MISTAKEN IDENTITY

JIM COOK (AS TOLD TO MARCIA HORNOK)

*Put on the whole armor of God, that you may
be able to stand against the wiles of the devil.*

EPHESIANS 6:11 NKJV

When we lived in Illinois, my wife and I had two identical pure black cats. Fluffy was a gentle, good-natured house cat but liked the outdoors, too. The other cat joined our family later.

Outside our front door stood a huge elm tree, one hundred feet tall. In the spring, a couple of blue jays moved into that tree and built their nest. As soon as they had eggs to guard, they viewed our poor cat as their number one enemy. She went out the door one day and got dive-bombed. Fluffy jumped and ran for cover. The jays continued to attack whenever Fluffy came into the front yard. Soon she was afraid to go outside at all.

Around this time we acquired our second black cat, a semi-feral who lived under the house across the street. The renters there moved away and abandoned her.

I started feeding her, and she got used to me. We named her Mama Kitty. When we brought her into our home, we had "twin" cats.

The first time Mama Kitty went out the front door, however, the jays must have thought it was easy-prey Fluffy. One of them zoomed down for the attack. Mama Kitty wasn't the least bit intimidated. She stuck out her front paw as the jay zeroed in, and with one swipe, batted him away. The jays never bothered either cat again.

Watching Mama Kitty triumph over the enemy by extending one little paw made me think of the line from Martin Luther's hymn, "A Mighty Fortress Is Our God." In his stanza about this world filled with devils, he says they should not make us fear or tremble because God's truth will triumph. Satan's doom is certain—"One little word shall fell him."

In fact, scripture never says Christians have to flee from Satan or his demons. Satan flees from us when we resist him (see James 4:7). God tells us to arm ourselves so we can stand against the devil and his principalities. In Ephesians 6:11–14 the word *stand* occurs four times: "stand against the wiles of the devil. . .withstand in the evil day, and having done all, to stand. Stand therefore. . ." (NKJV). Because the Holy Spirit in us is greater than any of Satan's forces in the world (see 1 John 4:4), we should not be intimidated by anything we perceive to be satanic or demonic. Even though the devil seeks to devour us, we can resist him with steadfast faith (see 1 Peter 5:8–9).

Fluffy didn't know one little swat could fell a blue jay, so she lived in fear of them. Mama Kitty stood her ground and raised her paw. Let's be like Mama Kitty whenever we face the enemy's temptations and attacks.

WAKING UP IS SO HARD TO DO

DEE ASPIN

My help comes from the Lord, who made heaven and earth. . . .
He who keeps you will not slumber.

PSALM 121:2–3 RSV

Tigger has a daily routine to wake his mistress, Kim, every morning when he wakes up on the pillow next to her head. First, he crawls closer to Kim's body, stretches his whole paw out over her nose, and squeezes her nose gently, as if he were holding a Kleenex. Then if she still doesn't wake up, he projects one claw from the same paw and gently taps it on the bridge of her nose. He keeps tapping, gradually increasing in strength—as if he were an impatient person tapping his nails on a counter—until she wakes up acknowledging him with a good morning massage.

Erika's cat, Chena, knows morning wake-up is the most difficult time for her mistress, too. So at first she gently pads around her head, back and forth on the pillow as if she were tracing and retracing a silhouette. If the slumbering giant remains motionless, she amps up her legs and moves faster and faster from side to side, adding a raspy purr for special effect. Erika awakens from her dreams as though she had been on a night sleeper in a roaring twenties railroad compartment as the engine shakes and sputters into a platform—its first stop of the day. And she is alert enough to shake, rattle, and roll out of bed.

Recently Judith's new cat did something none of her cats ever had! She hit the bed from the floor with a super-cat hurdle and then plopped straight onto Judith's face—claws extended. Judith woke with a painful *ouch!* She reached up and touched her forehead, bleeding from the puncture wound. After cleaning off her first battle scar of the day, she surmised, "She must have forgotten to retract her claws. She has been pretty ruffled lately with the other cats."

Thankfully we don't have to devise some clever strategy each morning to wake up our Creator. We are assured He is going to care for our watering, feeding, safety, and general well-being. We can pray or cry for help at any time of the day or night, and we know He hears. Our Creator never slumbers or sleeps. He does not check out for a while to replenish Himself, like we—His critters—need to do regularly.

We need never worry about hurting our heavenly Father with words or a terrible entrance because of life's aggravations. He knows our situation better than we do. If we have had a recent fight with a prowling enemy or we are frantic to find safety, God is always awake and waiting to help us.

We can rest each night, knowing He will continue to watch over us when we sleep, just as much as when we are stirring about during the day. Just as we watch over our animals most of the time. . .except when we are catnapping.

ENEMIES AT THE TABLE

DAVID WANDERING

You prepare a table before me in
the presence of my enemies.

PSALM 23:5 NIV

Arwen was a misfit cat in the Philippines. Even though he was an adopted stray into our American missionary home, he was *not* a Filipino cat—or at least he didn't see himself as one. Most cats in the Philippines have a status on par with the rodents they catch. Even though Arwen was just your average tabby alley cat, our Filipino friends would comment how nice his fur was and ask what breed he was (to our amusement!). To their surprise, we would then tell them that we fed him American cat food and that's the reason he looked so healthy.

Like most cats, Arwen enjoyed eating but was a picky eater. Even though he was just a stray Filipino cat, Arwen obviously saw himself as king of our home. And he enjoyed this status without much competition—except when it came to his food. Sometimes Arwen would not eat all his food, leaving some in his dish for a later snack. He never, however, had the chance to finish his leftovers. Nightly, a giant bullfrog would squeeze its way under our screen door and help himself to Arwen's cat food in his dish. He would gobble up Arwen's food and then sit in the drinking water of the cat dish. This was one smart frog! Every time we shooed him away, he would return the next evening. It was like he was visiting his nightly bed and breakfast. Arwen had a pesky enemy.

Arwen, of course, did not like the fact that a giant frog finished off his food every night. But instead of chasing it away, he would just stare at it and then treat the frog with indifference. I thought that Arwen's cat instincts would surely kick in and he would give chase to this enemy, but he never did. So night after night, the bullfrog returned and feasted on Arwen's food. He let his enemy get the best of him.

God has also prepared a table before us in the presence of our enemies. But we need not look on them with indifference or be intimidated by them. We are His royal children and have every right to the blessings of the King of kings. Let's not allow our enemy to steal our blessings right from under our noses. Instead, let's claim our rightful inheritance and delight in the daily feast God has prepared for us. It is ours, free for the taking!

GUARDED BY Attack CAtS

LYNNDA ELL

*For he will command his angels concerning
you to guard you in all your ways.*

PSALM 91:11 NIV

One Saturday evening, the two cats and I were in the living room, watching TV. George, my American shorthair, dozed on the sofa. Chloé, my petite Abyssinian, lay in my lap, cleaning her face with one paw. I was relaxing after a day of hard work unpacking boxes in our new home.

With no advance notice, both cats sat up and looked toward the other end of the house. They jumped down and took off down the hall in full hunt mode, running with bellies low to the floor. This was strange behavior for two house cats who never went outside, never hunted anything larger than a fly.

Quietly I followed them into the darkened bedroom to discover the reason for their actions. When I entered the room, I saw them both sitting on their haunches—side by side—looking at the windows in the wall facing the alley. Through the partially closed blinds, I could see a man walking down the alley, where he had no reason being.

I quickly dialed 911 and told the operator that someone was trying to break into my house. We exchanged the necessary information and she alerted the police to my emergency.

To this day, I do not know what prompted her next question. She said, "Ma'am, are you scared?"

Rather indignantly, I answered, "Well of course I'm scared! I'm alone in the house and my only means of protection are this phone and two house cats." I could not be sure, but I thought I heard a sputter of laughter.

The truth was that I *was* scared, but not panicked. I knew that God was protecting me. My confidence in Him must have revealed itself in the way I was speaking.

While all this was taking place, my faithful guard cats continued sitting between the man moving around in the alley and me. They followed the man's progress by moving their heads in unison, always facing exactly where he stood.

Just as suddenly as it had started, it was all over. George and Chloé calmly got up and headed back to the living room. They knew the man had left, so I no longer needed them to protect me. Less than five minutes later, the police arrived and verified that the prowler was gone.

It may seem a little strange that my pets would act more like guard dogs than house cats. However, cats acting out of character to protect me are no stranger than crows feeding a prophet. We may not always see the angels God provides for our protection, but on that Saturday night, my angels had furry feet and a purr.

$\int t A N \mathcal{P} \overset{\circ}{I} N G \; \int t \overset{\circ}{I} L L$

SARA FOUST

And Moses said unto the people, Fear ye not, stand still,
and see the salvation of the LORD, which he will shew to you to day.

EXODUS 14:13 KJV

When Willow was a kitten, she seemed afraid of virtually everything from people and loud noises to a small stuffed cat that made a soft purring noise when moved. After I adopted her and brought her home (leaving the stuffed cat behind), she seemed to adjust to life with her new family quickly.

She was curious about her surroundings and investigated anything new that appeared around the house. Every time I brought home groceries, she would come to see what new foods and boxes I had purchased.

After arriving home from the store one day, I carried in all of our groceries, placed each bag on the kitchen floor, and began unpacking them. Willow awoke from her nap on the couch, stretched, and started snooping through the bags, sticking her little pink nose into each bag one at a time.

When she failed to find anything interesting in the first few bags she decided to actually stick her entire head into the next bag. Unfortunately, when she inserted her head into this bag, the loop handle became stuck around her neck. I had emptied the bag already and so, when she pulled back, the bag came with her. I saw the same fear enter her eyes that I had seen when she was a kitten. She panicked and started backing blindly toward the kitchen table. The faster Willow tried to escape her pursuer, the louder the plastic bag rattled.

I realized that while I found this situation somewhat amusing, she was terrified of this horrible monster clinging to her neck. She ran around the living room for a few minutes dragging the noisy bag behind her. I tried to catch her in order to help her, but she was so scared that she was even avoiding me, so I had no choice but to stand back and watch what she would do. Finally, though, she did stop in the middle of the floor and looked to me for help.

She seemed to suddenly understand that she could not fix this situation by running away in fear and she allowed me to remove the bag.

Willow was not harmed, and I had gained a new insight. When we are faced with a situation in which we are afraid, if we can stand still and let God help us through, then we will escape unharmed. Our devils and fears chase us just as the bag was "chasing" Willow. But we will never be able to run fast enough to escape all of our fears and sins. Therefore, the only answer that makes any real sense is to turn to God for His all-knowing help. He will always be there for us and show us the *right* direction, even when we have been running in the wrong one.

While Willow may never investigate a plastic grocery bag again, if we stand still and let God work in our lives, we *can* face all of our fears.

B. B. the Siamese

Meredith LeBlanc

The righteous are bold as a lion.

Proverbs 28:1 NASB

I was living on a forty acre farm on Brindley Mountain in Alabama with three little boys, two dogs, three barn cats, and assorted livestock. There was plenty to take care of, but I felt a huge desire for a Siamese cat. I finally located a breeder and bought a beautiful male, sable colored with chocolate markings and startling blue eyes.

We named him B. B. He was to be my pet and live in the house. I furnished him with a soft bed, toys, and a beautiful set of porcelain bowls for food and water. B. B. would live a life of ease and experience luxury the barn cats could only dream of.

I was drawn to Siamese cats because I had read about their legendary voice. They are great communicators. They are also very people oriented. I just knew I would be in store for a constant companion.

Little did I know how much our menagerie of animals would

affect B. B. He had been with me for just a few days when he met the barn cats. He was instantly challenged to lead this pack of wild things. He stalked, herded, and voiced his commands in that distinctive voice as only a Siamese can. Although I tried to coax him back to the safety of the house, he was adamant. B. B. had found his calling.

I was frightened for him. The older cats were wild, used to the confines of the barn. Their daily activity consisted of lurking about the premises on the lookout for unwanted vermin. They traveled together and came and went as they pleased. They were not the likes I wanted my B. B. to associate with.

From that day on, B. B. was changed. My dream of a beautiful pet that was faithful to me was crushed. With a heart of lion, he braved all the dangers of the farm with his pack of followers. The chickens and the guinea hens respected them; the cows and pigs feared them. The animals weren't terrorized, only kept in line for the sake of peace and harmony.

In time B. B. fathered a litter of kittens with one of the barn cats. I am not sure how he managed, but he was able to get the mama in the wood box that opened inside the family room. It was there that she gave birth to the most beautiful babies. He came back into the house for the first time in months. He was a proud parent who guarded his family.

B. B. loved his role of protecting, leading, and loving his followers. He is a model of our heavenly Father, our Lion of Judah. Just as B. B. was being a testament to his heritage, a cat with a huge heart for his mission, God wants us to have that same calling. We can have the heart of a lion through the Holy Spirit that indwells us.

†HE REŞCUE

LYNNDA ELL

[God says] "He will call upon me, and I will answer him;
I will be with him in trouble, I will deliver him."

PSALM 91:15 NIV

Hearing the desperate cries, Julie looked around for the hungry kittens. She backtracked along the raised gravel path near the school, peering down into the weed-and-trash strewn ditches. Local pedestrians eyed her curiously; they showed no interest in the desperate cries, only in the strange behavior of the white American woman. Children gathered to watch her as she hitched her backpack a little higher and slid down into the deep ditch. Stepping carefully, watching for snakes, spiders, and other creepy-crawlies, she searched for the source of the cries.

There! Separating the weeds and dropping to one knee, Julie peered down at three tiny kittens. Two of them were huddled together, shivering with fright and hunger. The piercing cries were coming from the third kitten standing defiantly beside the other two. Their hair matted and their bodies gaunt from hunger, the kittens looked like their mother had abandoned them—or something had killed her. That happened often to feral cats in Guinea-Bissau, the West African nation where Julie was teaching in the Peace Corps.

The ladies who sold snacks by the side of the school strained to see what she was doing as she set down her backpack and cleared space in the smaller compartment to carry the kittens. Gently she picked up the two quiet kittens and put them in the pouch. She scooped up the noisy one who immediately began hissing and spitting at her. That stopped as she placed the kitten in the backpack with her sisters. Julie settled her backpack in place and then scrambled up to the path.

The children crowded around her. "What have you got?" they asked.

"Baby kittens."

One of the snack ladies giggled behind the hand that covered her mouth.

"Are you going to eat them?"

Everyone thought that was funny, for who knew what one of those crazy Americans would do.

"No, I'm not going to eat them!" Julie acted outraged, knowing it was part of the game. Becoming more serious she said, "I'm taking them home so that I can try to make them feel better."

Now a new cry went up from the snack ladies and the children. "Take us home, too, and make us feel better!"

"I don't have room for all of you, just for these tiny kittens!"

"Oh, well," they agreed, "maybe next time."

Isn't that the way Jesus rescued us from our sin-filled life? We were totally rejected, frightened, abandoned, and unloved. Everyone else ignored our condition. He heard our desperate cries and *not counting the cost*, He rescued us by taking the punishment for our sins on the cross.

The most amazing news is that—like Julie with the kittens—our acceptance of Jesus as our Savior was only the beginning of the rescue. God promised in Psalm 91, He would hear us when we call. He's with you now, so why not tell Him what you need?

tHE SERPENt MEEtS HiS MAtCH

CHUCK MILLER

*Submit yourselves, then, to God. Resist the devil,
and he will flee from you.*

JAMES 4:7 NIV

Dad, come to the backyard. There's a snake back here!"

This was not a normal occurrence in our little yard. And the snake was big: green, white, and silver, at least two feet long. It started wriggling along the side of the house toward the front yard, and my son asked the most pertinent question: "Where's Baby?"

Baby is our misnamed gray inside-outside cat, who thinks he's not just king of the house, but king of the neighborhood. We've nicknamed him the "Gray Panther." And we knew he wouldn't be happy about a snake in his yard. Suddenly, there he was, investigating this new thing from a distance, tracking it along the side of the house. Then the snake disappeared.

My son called me again. The snake was in one of the thick, round bushes that line the front of our house. My son had seen the branches trembling; the snake looked funny in there. Then he asked again: "Where's Baby?" Neither one of us wanted the cat to tussle with a snake.

Suddenly we saw a gray blur under the bushes—and a green blur down the bush and rushing across the lawn: the snake making its getaway. In great haste. Life-or-death haste.

"Where's Baby?"

We looked around. Instantly Baby's head, like a frantic periscope, popped out of the top of the bush! He was looking for a way out—after he'd chased the snake away by going right up into the bush after it!

After reassuring Baby that he had done his job and the snake was gone, and taking a couple of pictures, we carefully pulled Baby from the bush. He wasn't at all happy about ending up in there. His blood was definitely up. But at least the snake was gone!

Going after the devil is like that. Resist him and he'll flee. We resist him with holiness, humility, obedience ("submit yourselves"), in the name of Jesus Christ. As the seventy-two disciples joyously marveled, "Lord, even the demons submit to us in your name" (Luke 10:17 NIV).

We must use the name of Jesus properly, however. Biblically, using someone's name means properly expressing his character, purposes, and authority. The name of Jesus is not a magic formula; the name means the whole person. It's like Joseph being given Pharaoh's signet ring in Genesis. He'd better use its authority wisely, in total trust, in ways that reflect well on the one who granted it.

Given all of that, we must still have the audacity to resist Satan, to track that old serpent down like Baby did, and roust him out no matter where he hides, in Jesus's name, with Jesus's character and power, and total trust.

And remember: It was from a bush that God originally revealed His name. A burning bush. And I'll bet the old serpent was a green blur fleeing that shrub, too!

tHE SURPRISE

LYNNDA ELL

I will lie down and sleep in peace, for you alone,
O LORD, make me dwell in safety.

PSALM 4:8 NIV

Chloé was a petite, mostly white Abyssinian. She had huge green eyes that seemed small under her oversized ears. Like a lynx's ears, they were feathered and tufted and enabled her to hear the quietest of sounds. The combination of large round eyes and jumbo ears gave her a waif-like look.

Chloé never outgrew her playful ways. She always acted like a two-year-old—constantly chattering, eternally curious, and trying to be the center of attention any time guests came to the house. Her joyful zest for life kept laughter bubbling up in me as she batted her favorite paper ball around the house and under the furniture.

From the time she arrived from Guinea-Bissau, Chloé's favorite place to sleep at night was cuddled close to my side. Almost every night, she purred us both to sleep. Because I sleep so soundly, that was usually the last sound I heard before the alarm clock went off at 6:00 a.m. the next morning.

One night, I woke in the middle of the night to feel Chloé playing with something on top of the covers of my bed. I tried to get her to leave her toy and settle at my side, but she refused. *Oh, well,* I thought, *she'll knock it off the bed in a minute and give it up.* It was wintertime and cold, so I didn't want to leave my nice warm bed to take her paper ball away from her.

As I lay there waiting for her to tire of playing by herself, I began to notice little sounds that were made when Chloé wasn't moving. Curious to see what she was doing, I reached up and turned on the lamp. There in the middle of the bed was a palmetto roach.

This bug looks like a regular roach, except that it is as long and as wide as a person's thumb. Most of the year, palmetto roaches live outside, but during winter, they attempt to come inside. Chloé had heard this one in the kitchen, looking for a warmer spot, and had decided it would make a very nice toy to play with on my bed.

I took vigorous exception to her opinion. As soon as I saw this very-much-alive roach scurrying across the covers, I threw them back and scrambled out of bed. I quickly picked up a book to smash the bug, but we couldn't find it. Unwilling to get back in the bed without knowing the exact location of that roach, I pulled a blanket out of the closet and spent the rest of the night on the sofa.

Chloé stole my peaceful night's rest with her antics. Other distractions may be stealing your slumber, but the answer is always the same: Trust in the Lord for a night of rest. He can keep you safe, regardless of the type of thief that wants to steal your sleep.

DAVID AND GOLIATH

KATHERINE A. FULLER

[David said,] The LORD that delivered me out of the paw of the lion, and out of the paw of the bear, he will deliver me out of the hand of this Philistine. And Saul said unto David, Go, and the LORD be with thee.

1 SAMUEL 17:37 KJV

My best friend from childhood had a little black cat named Woosie. We had some good times with that cat. She was a bundle of energy, playful, loving, and above all, a huntress. Not some scaredy-cat, as her name would suggest—not for her, the faint heart!

Woosie hunted the woods surrounding our neighborhood. This was her territory, and she guarded it with extreme vigilance. It was common to see her chasing birds, rabbits, field mice, and occasionally a stray cat. Nothing intimidated her—absolutely nothing.

I recall a particular day—all the kids were outside playing, taking advantage of the last warm days of autumn. Our riveting game of tag was halted abruptly by the appearance of a massive,

250-pound Saint Bernard. He was the classic medicine dog: dense coat of red and white fur, black face and ears, shaggy neck and legs, huge head, and large paws. His tail was long and heavy, hanging low with the end turned up. He even had a thick leather collar with a brandy barrel attached at his throat.

We scattered, screaming, our game forgotten. The mammoth canine was unfazed by our clamor and began exploring his new domain. He ambled along, smelling bushes, mailboxes, and the flagpole, marking each along the way. We climbed into trees and crowded into whatever shelters we could find so he could not get us.

Then Woosie came to our rescue. She came flying out of the woods—ears flattened, eyes flashing, howling like a banshee—and charged straight at the Saint Bernard. We watched as our little Woosie launched herself through the air, claws extended, straight at the dog's face.

He let out a startled yelp and jerked his head back, eyes showing white, and hightailed it out of there! It was a sight to see the Saint Bernard's lumbering gait as he whirled and hastily retreated. Excited, we scrambled out of our hiding places and gathered around our little hero, cheering and stroking her fur. Woosie just pointed her nose in the air, tail waving, and walked calmly away, as if to say, "Did you doubt me?"

David faced Goliath in much the same way. The armies of Israel cowered before the Philistine champion, and scattered when Goliath made his daily appearance to taunt them. David was small, but he was not intimidated by the giant's colossal frame or his threats. He wholeheartedly believed that God was big enough; that He would strengthen him for the battle—and that He would deliver Goliath to him, just as He had the bear and lion while

David tended his father's sheep.

We can have the same confidence that both Woosie and David had as we face the giants in our lives. Satan tries to intimidate, wear us out, and make us think that we are outclassed. But we have a God who always roots for, and supports, the undercat!

A CAT'S A CAT AND THAT'S THAT!: WISDOM

We should be careful to get out of an experience only the wisdom that is in it—and stop there; lest we be like the cat that sits down on a hot stove lid. She will never sit down on a hot stove lid again—and that is well; but also she will never sit down on a cold one anymore.

MARK TWAIN

tHE ALPHA FiGHt

LYNNDA ELL

*Pride only breeds quarrels, but wisdom is
found in those who take advice.*

PROVERBS 13:10 NIV

Spencer was definitely an alpha cat. He *thought* he was the alpha *person* in our household. He loved to lie in the flower boxes hanging off the balcony of our second floor apartment to watch the world go by beneath him.

Several times a week, the owner of a large, male Doberman pinscher would walk his dog down the sidewalk in front of our apartment. This Doberman had a superiority complex, too. He was a fine-looking animal: large noble head and shiny black coat with tan markings. He pranced down the sidewalk and growled around his leather muzzle as soon as he and Spencer caught each other's eye. Spencer was too cool to reply. The only thing he moved was his tail as he flicked it back and forth out of the dog's sight.

This state of affairs changed dramatically one Saturday morning. My husband was setting the table for breakfast when he looked up to see Spencer disappear over the end of the flower box. Immediately from below came the sounds of yelping and growling and cursing so mixed up together that it was hard to tell which was the dog and which the person.

My husband dropped the silverware and ran down the stairs. In front of the building was an irate man holding back his angry dog. Spencer crouched on the ground not far away, shaking his head to clear the blood from his nose. As my husband scooped up Spencer, the dog's owner proceeded to tell him in tones and words quite unkind, that we should keep our cat away from his dog because the dog might not be wearing a muzzle the next time.

My daughter, Julie, heard the rest of the story later that day. Spencer had jumped down on the back of the Doberman, sank his claws into him, and was biting the back of the dog's neck. The dog's owner, while trying to control the frantic dog, hit Spencer on the nose to make him let go of the dog, jerked him free of the dog by Spencer's collar, and then threw him out of the dog's reach.

Neither animal sustained any significant injury, although Spencer had a scar on his nose from the battle. The man and the Doberman never walked in front of our apartment again. That was also the last time Spencer went out on the balcony.

Spencer let his pride get him into a quarrel he could only lose. God protected him when the Doberman should have chewed him up. The next time our pride gets in the way of peace, we can remember Spencer and the alpha fight and then sit firmly on our pride.

EARLY MORNING SERENADE

ANNA M. AQUINO

But God hath chosen the foolish things of the world to confound the wise; and God hath chosen the weak things of the world to confound the things which are mighty.

1 CORINTHIANS 1:27 KJV

My dad worked long hours while I was growing up, and it wasn't uncommon for him to come home in the wee hours of the morning. My sister, while she was living at home, had a similar schedule. Both worked long hours and snuck into the house, trying not to wake the rest of us from our deep slumber.

On one particularly long day, around one in the morning, both my dad and sister arrived home within minutes of each other. It was so dark in the house that they were both trying to find their way around without tripping over their own two feet. Suddenly, they heard a noise that startled them. It sounded like an organ was playing. My sister figured it was me and was ready to give me the "what for" for playing our organ at such a ridiculous hour; and my dad was ready to get the baseball bat and knock out whomever the intruder happened to be.

As my sister made her way down the stairs to see who was playing the organ, my dad was also making his way around the corner to the same room. Both jumped into the music room from opposite ends.

"Aha!" my sister yelled.

"Hey!" yelled my dad.

To their surprise, it wasn't me they saw at the organ. It was Lynx, our gray long-haired cat, who'd somehow managed to turn on the keyboard with his paws and decided that one in the morning was the perfect time for a serenade. My sister and father laughed till the tears rolled, and Lynx's "Wee Hour of the Morning Melody" has become a family joke ever since.

Sometimes we look at God's Word and think that we know it all. It's easy to become arrogant in our faith, but sometimes God likes to remind us that we *don't* know everything. We can't consider ourselves so wise that we think we have nothing new to learn. And, if He must, God will use an organ-playing cat to remind us of that simple truth.

MAX AND MISS KITTY

DEE ASPIN

Let your "Yes" be yes, and your "No," no.

JAMES 5:12 NIV

In our neighborhood, cats are not allowed to roam free." I listened to Elizabeth recall the day she and Max, her handsome declawed blue point Siamese, paraded down the street in his royal blue harness, to call on his favorite feline.

Elizabeth knocked on the door. Max's taupe body tensed and his black nose twitched. Jayne, Miss Kitty's master, welcomed them inside. The visitors scanned the house from the entry hall and waited.

"Where's Miss Kitty?" No sooner had Elizabeth asked the question than a long-haired, black-and-white feline sauntered out, head held high. She walked past Elizabeth, turned slowly, and stopped a few feet from Max. Max's ears tilted back as he stepped quietly forward and faced Miss Kitty. He gazed into her creamy distant eyes for a moment and slowly pressed his lips on hers.

Jayne and Elizabeth winked at each other, entranced. They

had never seen Max kiss Miss Kitty. For a moment, the beautiful girl stood motionless before her suitor. Then, without a sound, she turned away, trotted past Elizabeth, and disappeared into the next room.

Max's turquoise eyes seemed to fade into forever. He stood still, transfixed. The grandfather clock ticking steadily from the living room seemed to chime with Max's heartbeat.

Moments later, Miss Kitty reappeared. Again she pranced by Elizabeth, assuming her position in front of Max. Elizabeth loosened the lead on Max's leash. Again the suitor pressed his lips on Miss Kitty's cherub mouth—and pulled away for his final gaze.

Miss Kitty picked up one paw and swatted Max swiftly on the cheek. He jerked back in surprise. Frowning, she turned and padded off.

Max, his eyes wide in unbelief, looked up to Elizabeth, dismayed. But Elizabeth and Jayne couldn't sympathize—they stood crying with laughter.

Haven't we all experienced Max's dismay at misunderstanding from poor communication between families, friends, peers at our workplace, or social circles?

I have worked in areas where management expected paperwork done according to policy and procedure that changed abruptly the next day. One moment what we are doing is right—the next moment it is wrong. It leaves us feeling puzzled when no explanation is given.

How many of us have had interpersonal relationships where we have been absolutely floored? We missed the feedback or misinterpreted the information from someone close to us. We said or behaved in a manner that was once acceptable and even encouraged by someone we connected with, only to discover what worked in the autumn disgruntles in winter?

When we look to God, dumbfounded by misunderstandings, He stands ready through His Holy Spirit to comfort, guide, and grant us insight as we pray. God knows our hearts. He can reveal when best to approach a person we have offended and how to speak truth in love.

Life challenges us to continue improving our communication skills. If we like something, say it. If we don't, let others know. If we're not sure, wait until we understand ourselves. Let our "yes" be yes and our "no" be no. When we flip back and forth too quickly, we confuse those around us. Just ask Max.

Spring Fever

DARLENE FRANKLIN

"Stand at the crossroads and look; ask for the ancient paths, ask where the good way is, and walk in it, and you will find rest for your souls. But you said, 'We will not walk in it.'"

JEREMIAH 6:16 NIV

Talia *loves* eating green grass. With the advent of spring rains and sprinklers, the lawns around my apartment turn positively lush. Even though she's an inside cat, Talia knows when springtime has come.

On a typical morning, I have to open the door pretty wide to exit with everything I have to carry. And as soon as Talia hears the locks tumble, she darts between my feet and out the door.

I have no ability to chase after a fast-acting cat, due to arthritis. . .nor do I have time, because I only open the door when I'm leaving home. What should I tell my boss? "The cat made me late" isn't a valid excuse.

But we play our game. I call Talia. She, of course, ignores me. I approach her. She slides under the railing, across the step, to grass on the other side. When I cross, she climbs where grass creeps between decorative boulders.

Then I take positive action. Balancing precariously on legs still recovering from knee surgery, I use my cane to hook Talia under her big belly. She wiggles away and squeezes through slats onto the patio. How she manages that feat, I'm never sure.

As a final resort, I go back inside, shutting the door behind me. Because, like cats everywhere, Talia *hates* closed doors—especially when it's the door that leads to her food dish. Usually that brings her running.

But when she's feasting on grass, even the closed-door trick doesn't work.

Talia, of course, doesn't understand why I don't want her outside. Cats make tasty tidbits for the coyotes and foxes that roam our suburban neighborhood. She might also get outside and never make it home again. After all, she was a stray when she was brought to the animal shelter.

All I can do is try to train her to stay inside. When I'm especially exasperated, I'll scold her, as if she can understand. "If you persist in going outside, I'll have to lock you in the bathroom before I leave, and *then* what kind of day will you have?"

All Talia understands is that I'm angry with her when she goes outside—something she considers a natural and even desirable destination.

Just as I know going outside is dangerous for Talia, God warns me about behaviors that could bring me harm. Also like my cat, I tend to ignore those warnings because I think I know better.

The next time God warns me about something, maybe I should listen.

tHE LEAP

LYNNDA ELL

A wise man fears the LORD and shuns evil,
but a fool is hotheaded and reckless.

PROVERBS 14:16 NIV

Spencer was an American shorthair cat who thought he was a full-mane African lion. Even the way he moved—that rolling shoulder walk, eyes searching ahead—looked leonine. He had that self-confident attitude that, for lack of a better word, I call *presence*. He lived up to his advertising, too. He assumed his rightful place in our household without being a bully and was friendly without being a nuisance.

He had one skill that always puzzled us. Without an obvious path, he could find a way to get to the highest perch in a room. His ability to leap unexpected heights and great lengths was a source of amazement. But his confidence in his jumping skills occasionally got him into trouble.

Spencer was an indoor cat. He had been neutered as soon as he was old enough and he seemed content to live indoors. We lived in a second floor apartment with a balcony that had flower boxes built into the railing. When the weather was nice, we would allow Spencer out on the balcony. He would promptly leap into the flower box and lie there in the sunshine, watching the world go by below him.

One particular spring day, Spencer had watched several fat, lazy pigeons eating crumbs on the lawn that fronted the building. When someone would walk by, the pigeons would fly up out of the way, circle back, and land again. The birds were aware of Spencer and were careful to keep what they thought was a safe distance from our balcony when they took off and landed. Finally, one pigeon got careless and came close enough for Spencer to take a flying leap out of the flower box and catch it in midflight, with nothing under the feline but fifteen feet of air.

I learned about this when my daughter, Julie, went screaming out of the apartment, flying down the stairs, to see if her cat was alive. When I looked over the balcony railing, I saw Julie on the ground beside a stunned, but conscious Spencer and a dead bird.

Julie carried Spencer, seemingly unaffected by his experience, back upstairs. He did not get to keep the bird, which I am sure disappointed him. It was a long time before he was allowed back out on the balcony.

Many times, I act like Spencer, recklessly depending on my own abilities to get me through a foolish activity. All the time, God wants me to seek Him and avoid evil. That is the very definition of a wise person. May God grant us enough common sense to learn to be wise.

tHE tALE OF tHREE KittiES

CONNIE PETERS

*"But whoever listens to me [wisdom] will live in
safety and be at ease, without fear of harm."*

PROVERBS 1:33 NIV

Karen's friend stood on her porch, watching her kitty play in the yard when an owl suddenly swooped down and caught the cat by its collar. The woman stood there in helpless horror, watching her panic-stricken pet take off into clear skies. Suddenly, the cat was in a free fall, hit the ground running, and disappeared under the porch. The cat's plastic collar had snapped in the bird's sharp talons.

Karen, keeping this story in mind, decided when she got three kittens, she'd keep them indoors, free from marauding owls and other hungry critters. Giuseppe, Murphy, and Sid might not know the pleasures of chasing field mice and butterflies, but they'd be safe. Or so she thought.

They lived a life of luxury: free reign of the house, the best food, and lots of kitty toys to keep them busy. Giuseppe, fluffy, orange, and adorable, won everyone's heart. Murphy, also orange, was a curious cat and enjoyed playing with his kitty friends. Sid, the practical cat, looked like Morris of the cat-food commercial fame. He was the wise guy and treated Giuseppe and Murphy with condescension.

One evening when Karen came home from work, she knew something was wrong. Giuseppe was meowing his little kitty head off, and Sid and Murphy were nowhere to be seen.

Giuseppe-turned-Lassie led Karen down the stairs where Sid had his head stuck in a plastic sack. He must have tried to back his way out of the bag—the whole way down the steps, across the cellar floor, and into the corner. One cat found—alive, distraught, but well.

Karen searched *everywhere* for Murphy: all through the cellar, in each room on the main floor, and even outside. She started looking in crazy places: in drawers, under the couch, even in the bathtub. At last, she found him in the kitchen. Murphy must have been so distressed about Sid's predicament that he fell from the stovetop and wedged in between the stove and the wall like a hapless hiker in a fissure. Murphy and Sid had no strength left to meow, but Giuseppe had done enough caterwauling for the three of them.

We can try our best to keep ourselves and loved ones safe from expected dangers, but there are always those unexpected ones like being caught in a plastic bag, falling behind the stove, or being snatched up by an owl. Ultimately, we need to rely on God by praying for His wisdom and protection, which may come in the form of a caterwauling friend.

CATS' FEET ON LOW PLACES

GAYLE LINTZ

Surely God is good to Israel, to those who are pure in heart. But as for me, my feet had almost slipped; I had nearly lost my foothold.

PSALM 73:1–2 NIV

A couple of times each day, when T-Tat is bored, she entices me to play with her. She'll hunker down, give a sideways peek, and wait for me to take a step toward her. When I take that step, she races away, makes a sharp turn into the next room, and waits for me to chase her. That worked wonderfully well in our old apartment. In the new place, it's a different story.

The previous apartment was carpeted throughout. At the new one, only the bedroom has carpet, and it's a "No Cat" zone. The rest of the rooms have hardwood floors. The chase games have changed.

Now when I step toward the crouching cat, she leaps up and pumps her legs, expecting to sprint to the living room door. But she doesn't. She looks like cats in cartoons. You remember the scenes, where the cats are suspended for a few seconds while their legs gyrate at full tilt, then they speed off. T-Tat struggles several moments before she can gain purchase and run. Then, she races to the door, swings her body sideways, and tries to jump to make the tight turn into the living room. But the slippery floor turns her paws into skates on ice. She glides on down the hallway, past her target, often bumping into a piece of furniture or the wall.

T-Tat is very excited when my wife or I arrive home, whether the absence was lengthy or we just stepped out to take the trash to the curb. One of her favorite welcome-home antics is to zip through the living room and leap onto a chair, where she waits for us to come rub her head and greet her with those "Oh, kitty, kitty, kitty" noises cat owners make. That's not working all too well, either. She will race up to the chair, plant her hind legs, and stretch her upper body out to leap. But the planting doesn't work. Instead, her hindquarters keep on going, sliding out from under her. She executes a lovely cat backflip and seems confused. Why is she still on the floor, instead of up on the chair?

We've lived here for months, but her behavior hasn't changed. Maybe the desire for speed outweighs any inclination to learn a different way of moving through the apartment. Or maybe she just likes this new slipping, sliding, and slamming through the place.

The world is changing in amazing ways these days. At our home, we don't have a landline, relying instead on our cell phones. We don't have a television set, but I watch some shows each week, online. As a graphic designer, much of my work involves creating web sites for individuals and businesses. My career didn't even exist when I was born thirty years ago. While we know that all things are gifts from God, how people use those things is a different matter. We need to be careful that we don't lose our foothold as we navigate through life today.

A COOL CAT:
CONTENTMENT

I wish I had the contentment of my kitty who,
while industrious in his own way, understands the
importance of taking a nap or curling up beside someone
important to him or enjoying a spot of sun on the
floor before it moves on with the day.
CAROL SMITH

tiGGER'S FAVORiTE ROOM

DEE ASPIN

*The LORD is good to all; he has
compassion on all he has made.*

PSALM 145:9 NIV

Everybody has a favorite room in the house. Tigger the tabby's room happens to be the bathroom. It didn't take Kim long to discover her rescue cat had an affection for water.

When Kim bathed in the tub, Tigger eagerly perched on the edge, staring intently into the water as if it were a great fishing hole. That is, until he realized the personal benefits bathtub water could provide. Kim winced at the horrible screeches Tigger sometimes made while she was bathing—until one day she discovered what drove him to make the awful sounds.

She dipped her hand into the bathwater and cupped it until she wet his head. He continued the meow howl. Then she decided to try and scoop up more water. This time she wet his head, neck, and back, giving him a sponge bath fit for Puss 'n Boots. He stopped his call of the wild and purred contentedly. "Tigger had been feeling dirty and once he felt like he was clean, he was one happy kitty."

She discovered the secret code to transform her disgruntled screecher into a prancing, contented cat. And although the toilet water doesn't contain the natural homeopathic cures of the bathtub basin, it does provide a source of study for the adventurous side of Tigger.

Kim noted that Tigger always liked to stare, mesmerized at the rapidly circulating water in her porcelain cylinder after a good flush, as if it were a river whirlpool ready to pop up something from the rich depths of the hole.

One day as Kim stood washing her hands at the sink, Tigger stood beside her on his back legs, with his right paw on the toilet rim and his left paw on the lever of the toilet. He pushed down forcefully with his left paw, trying to emulate Kim's swift successful flush—only moments earlier. Nothing happened. His strength was not that of his master. Only once, months later, did Kim again catch Tigger in the same place, same position, and with the same unsuccessful results on the toilet handle.

How many of us have felt disturbed by residue from a misadventure? We seek our Master for cleansing, too. But unlike Kim, God already knows we need a thorough wash. He already made the way through the cross and forgiveness of Christ when we come to Him. And when our souls are washed by God's truth and His Word, we are set free from the sticky stuff.

How many times do we fritter away our energy, attempting to do something that we were not created to do? God can make a river hole—but we'll never figure it out. Maybe we can enjoy our corner of the world as much as Tigger if we know when to sit back and enjoy the water holes and when to stop striving, keeping our paws off the levers of life that only our Master can operate.

FLYING HIGH

BETTY OST-EVERLEY

If we confess our sins, he is faithful and just and will forgive us our sins and purify us from all unrighteousness.

1 JOHN 1:9 NIV

H appy anniversary, sweetheart!"

My husband presented me with a beautiful arrangement of colorful alstroemeria and bright stargazer lilies, a reminder of my wedding bouquet of nine years earlier. In the center of the arrangement was a green ribbon tied to a shiny Mylar balloon, HAPPY ANNIVERSARY printed on one side.

A couple of weeks later, I deposited the spent blossoms in the compost pile but held on to the balloon, which had deflated only slightly, a remembrance of my husband's thoughtfulness. At one end of the bright ribbon was the balloon; the other, a plastic disk used to keep it anchored to an earthbound existence. Sometimes, air from a vent would move it from hovering over the dining room table. The disk would dip downward periodically toward the floor, a newfound curiosity to my three cats.

Two of the cats, Yoda and Chewbacca (whom we usually call Chewy), were unusually fascinated with a disk that seemed to appear out of nowhere. Its strange mobility perplexed them, and especially so when they batted at it.

After a week or so of pawing and batting at a suspended disk, Chewy found that he could lead the balloon if he took the ribbon in his mouth. My husband and I exploded in laughter at the sight of a solid black behemoth taking a balloon for a walk. When he came to a doorway, Chewy was further confused by the balloon's unwillingness to follow.

By the end of the week, Chewy had mastered balloon-walking. However, the foil balloon deflated more and more by the day, partially due to its age and being consistently dragged through doorways. It began to hang a little lower.

One afternoon Chewy decided to take his balloon for another walk, but it flew much closer to the floor than usual. It was then he realized that a silver object was following him! His walk turned into a run as he tried to escape from the unidentified flying object. The balloon was still behind him. Chewy ran under the coffee table, the balloon banging underneath as it followed. This noise made Chewy travel faster, and, of course, so did the balloon. The cat darted behind the sofa and the balloon got caught between another piece of furniture, yanking the plastic disk from Chewy's mouth. Chewy responded by hiding under the dining room table. The balloon was flattened, which marked the end of balloon-chasing and balloon-walking.

We sometimes hold on to balloons of our own. We become mired in sin and guilt, not releasing them when we should. Our Father has given us the remedy for not having sin and guilt follow and hang over us like a balloon. The remedy is to confess our sins to Him. He is faithful to forgive us, which allows our sins to fly away. Do you have guilt hanging over your head?

†HE BRIGHt AND
SHINY †HINGS

DEE ASPIN

*The LORD is compassionate and gracious,
slow to anger, abounding in love.*

PSALM 103:8 NIV

Darlene had a young cat named Tiger, an adventurous hunter who loved to bring gifts home. Tiger found a great place to store her collection and proudly display them—inside her family's boots. Darlene, her husband, and children learned to check before absently thrusting their toes into the depths of their boots lest they squash the dead tiny creatures—critters with long tails tucked inside like pesky shoestrings.

Tiger concentrated on her second favorite sport—climbing trees.

On Tiger's first Christmas, Darlene hosted the family gathering at their holiday house. She set the table for an elaborate turkey dinner with all the trimmings on her finest china. Everyone sat devouring the delicious holiday meal, when suddenly activity stopped. A visitor pointed, her fork midair. All eyes riveted to the Christmas tree. It moved.

As they studied the tree closely, suddenly two bright shiny eyes appeared glowing from the top of the Douglas fir—an almost perfect tree topper. Unfortunately, this live wire was too heavy and active for that prestigious position. The festive tree swayed precariously. Not to be fooled, Tiger had identified the inviting green branches underneath all the blinking lights and shiny ornaments, as a real tree—and a challenging new climb.

Various family members darted from the table to circumvent impending disaster and caught the tree before it toppled over. Stunned by all the commotion, Tiger ran down the trunk and out of sight, never to climb a Christmas tree again. She returned to her love of hunting and continued to provide the family with presents throughout the year.

Like Tiger, we sometimes think we are blessing others when we may not be doing that at all. If we take off to catch some fish for grilling, when those we love do not like fish and would rather be with us, it's more about us and what we like. When we take the time to know people, we find out what they are interested in and what encourages them and makes them smile. If we live in pursuit of risk and adventure, we may overlook the possibility of problems—including compromising our own safety and creating distress to those close to us.

Life offers lots of shiny ornaments and lighted trees to enamor us that at first appear genuine. Sometimes we are attracted to the glitz and glamour of something new, thinking it will provide true satisfaction and a good experience.

But after we try clinging to anything—or anyone—with shallow roots, we realize leaning on a false foundation will not satisfy and can even be dangerous. Simple pleasures can bring us happiness if we are content, expectant, and observant of the world God has placed us in. Just like the deeply rooted evergreens outside of Tiger's Christmas house provide a good view and safe perch.

As Darlene overlooked Tiger's curious antics, hopefully we can overlook those around us. Together we learn about the bright and shiny things, even as God oversees our growth and the lessons we learn under His loving eyes!

ESCAPE?

LYNNDA ELL

He has given us his very great and precious promises, so that. . .
you may. . .escape the corruption in the world caused by evil desires.

2 PETER 1:4 NIV

Spencer was the stereotype of a lion. He may have looked like a house cat, but he didn't act like one. He bonded with my younger daughter, Julie. However, he intimidated my older daughter, letting her know she was not the alpha "cat." He enjoyed harassing her, jumping on her from around a corner, chasing her down the hallway, biting her ankles if she walked too near. . .

Spencer believed that being domesticated was okay, if it didn't get in the way of what he wanted to do, which was escape the apartment. He was too proud to crowd around our feet and dart out of the door. He was too smart to think that would be a successful method of escape. Nevertheless, he did escape; and the first time he got out, I thought one of the girls had failed to close the door properly.

"Julie," I yelled over the balcony, "look for Spencer! The door was left open and he got out."

Julie and her friends quickly searched the stairwell, recovered the cat, and returned him to the apartment. Julie also firmly denied leaving the door open.

One afternoon not too long after Spencer had started escaping, I heard some scratching noises on the landing outside the door. I opened it to see Spencer playing with a mouse between the doors of the two apartments. When I opened the door, Spencer became distracted just long enough for the mouse to escape and to squeeze under my neighbor's door.

I scooped up Spencer and knocked on the door. As soon as it opened, I said, "I'm sorry, but a mouse ran into your apartment."

Stepping in and looking around, I spotted the mouse under the dining room table. While wrestling the twisting, yowling, angry ball of fur in my arms, I quickly got between the dining room table and the door to the kitchen. My neighbor ran for her broom, and her two children started jumping up and down and squealing. It was just too much for the poor little mouse. He dashed out the door and down the stairs.

As you can imagine, our neighbors were angry at Spencer's mouse-catching efforts. We promised to keep a closer eye on him. However, he continued to get out of the house, and we didn't know how he did it. Eventually, we discovered that Spencer was opening the door himself by jumping off a nearby bookshelf and holding down the door handle. From then on, we always kept the door locked.

Spencer's desire to escape the apartment led him into risky situations, but he was determined to have his own way. The next time you want to escape from your circumstances, do a quick check of your desires. If they are selfish ones, you may find that, just like Spencer, getting what you want causes you even more problems than you had before.

WHERE'S OUR CAT?

GAYLE LINTZ

*You are my hiding place; you will protect me from trouble
and surround me with songs of deliverance.*

PSALM 32:7 NIV

We moved.

For weeks, we cleaned out cabinets and drawers. We packed boxes and bags. We evaluated our furnishings, much of which had been scavenged from the streets around our Brooklyn apartment. Several pieces went back out onto the street.

T-Tat was curious, snooping into piles and boxes and finding new places to snooze. My wife charmed the grocery store owner around the corner, and we made several trips to our new place, rolling our boxes down the street in a couple of borrowed carts.

The last weekend, a friend loaned us his SUV, and we transported the few pieces of furniture we were keeping. On the final trip over, we took T-Tat and her things.

Transition is hard for everyone. T-Tat cautiously picked her way around cartons, located her food and water bowls in the new kitchen, and tried out the windowsill that looked out over the new backyard.

A couple of mornings after the move, I couldn't find the cat. Bathroom? No. Under the sofa? No. In any windowsill? No. Waiting outside the closed bedroom door, just in case we had changed the no-cats-in-the-bedroom rule in the new place? Again, no.

I feared we had left a door open, but both were shut and locked. Where was the cat?

Finally, I resorted to the classic fallback maneuver of cat owners everywhere. I went into the kitchen and jiggled her food bowl, as though I was putting out fresh food. She appeared immediately, which did not surprise me. But I was quite startled by where she appeared from. She had plunged to the floor from above me. Where had she been? Napping on the fridge?

Later, unpacking and finding places for our belongings, I again missed T-Tat. I went back to the kitchen and checked the top of the refrigerator. Nope. But, with a closer look, I did notice, way up in the 8-inch space between the ceiling and the cabinet tops, a couple of furry gray cat ears.

"T-Tat?" I called softly. No response. I jiggled her bowl. Down she flew. It seemed unfair to trick her that way again, so she got a couple of cat treats.

Poor girl. All the parts of her life had changed. Everything looked different and smelled different and *was* different. So, she went looking for a safe place to retreat, away from the disarray and disorganization, where things were quiet, and sometimes, if you waited long enough, people put food in your bowl.

Lives are full of things that make us search for a haven of rest. A shift in jobs or relationships or financial status can make us feel insecure. But God is with us through constancy and change. When we feel overwhelmed, we do have a Hiding Place, and Someone who will surround us with songs of deliverance, which can be just as satisfying as a handful of kitty treats.

WHAT'S EATING YOU?

Marcia Hornok

"Why do you spend money for what is not bread, and your wages for what does not satisfy? Listen carefully to Me, and eat what is good, and delight yourself in abundance."

Isaiah 55:2 NASB

My friend Kim has a morbidly obese cat. When he lies on his side, he looks like a bagpipe. It used to take him several attempts to summit a sofa cushion. Now he doesn't even try.

Kim rescued Willie from the street when he was three or four weeks old. She does not know how he became stranded from his mother while still nursing, but Kim bottle-fed the scrawny starving kitten until he thrived.

As Willie grew up, he became a food addict. Unlike other cats that leave food in their bowl, Willie ate up every morsel and looked for more, as if determined never to starve again.

I don't know if cats have emotional needs, but Willie obviously has a hunger that must hearken back to his childhood deprivation. Consequently he now has liver problems, a kind of feline diabetes.

We may rightly ask, "What's eating Willie that makes him want to eat?" We'll never know, but don't we have the same problem? We all grow up with holes in our souls from childhood hurts. Some of us deal with extreme atrocities while others experienced minor losses. We often try to fill these voids with overindulgence, even to the point of addiction. We think that temporary pleasures from excessive eating, buying, working, or playing will satisfy our craving, but it only creates more hunger.

When we become emotionally obese from self-indulgence, we are like Pharisees who sought spiritual life from rules and rituals rather than from relationship with God. Jesus told them, "You are unwilling to come to Me so that you may have life" (John 5:40 NASB).

I'm guilty as charged. When a problem confronts me, many times I've called up friends before taking it to the Lord in prayer. Reading self-help books and how-to magazine articles often replaces seeking comfort, hope, and guidance from the scriptures. And when I feel like I deserve something I'm not getting, I can eat potato chips and dip like I'm out of control.

Are you like that, too? We all need to come to Christ with our destructive habits every time we're tempted. Ask Him to help us stop indulging the flesh because we feel deprived in spirit. Instead of spending money, time, and worry seeking temporal satisfaction, let us retrain ourselves to "eat what is good" from God's Word and delight ourselves in Him.

Like Willie, we can form harmful habits to heal past hurts, or we can eat freely of the spiritual bread of God's abundance and be satisfied.

FRANTIC FELINE

Jo Upton

Trust God from the bottom of your heart; don't try to figure out everything on your own. Listen for God's voice in everything you do, everywhere you go; he's the one who will keep you on track.

Proverbs 3:5–6 msg

Puddin' was a petite, multicolored cat with a sweet disposition and a happy-go-lucky attitude that made her special, if only to us. She wasn't a beautiful cat; in fact she wasn't exceptional in any particular way; that is, until she had kittens.

Puddin' really took to motherhood. Unlike some cats, she seemed to sense this was a higher calling. She was determined to protect and provide for this little brood, no matter how difficult the task. The kittens were born in a comfy box, which we placed inside a large wooden storage building with windows. The area also served as a playhouse for our daughter, so it had a few cushioned chairs and boxes of toys our children had outgrown. After the last kitten was born, we left the new mom and babies resting quietly, certain that we had provided safe accommodations.

Apparently Puddin' didn't agree. When we returned to feed her, we found the box empty. After a desperate search, we found she had moved to another box, one filled with stuffed animals. A quick head count showed that several kittens were missing. Muffled cries told us they were on the bottom of the box, covered with a mountain of toys. We carefully took them out and placed each one back in the original box.

At the next feeding, we found she had once more moved the kittens, this time to a dangerously high shelf. We brought them down, placed them on a blanket in the middle of the floor near several clean boxes, and left. We hoped she might choose one of the boxes and put the kittens in without our meddling. But by the next day, we watched in horror as Puddin' climbed down the side of the building, a full 12 feet high, with a screaming kitten in her mouth. She was apparently on her way to find another "safe" spot for her family.

This went on for weeks. We were constantly trying to undo Puddin's misguided attempts at protecting her family. Why did she continually relocate the kittens and risk hurting them? She thought she knew best, but her logic was flawed. She didn't see the big picture and never realized the unwanted outcome her decisions might cause.

Unless we heed the advice in Proverbs, we could spend much of our life like Puddin'—rushing down the wrong path, hoping to arrive at the right place. God knows that even our best tries, apart from His leading, will turn out badly. But if we listen to His voice and allow Him to direct our steps, we will remain on track. That's just the kind of comfort and assurance that we all need and only God can provide!

SPACE INVADERS

CONNIE PETERS

*Thou art worthy, O Lord, to receive glory and honour and power:
for thou hast created all things, and for thy pleasure
they are and were created.*

REVELATION 4:11 KJV

I'm invaded by Snickers—not the candy bar, but my calico cat. Maybe because when she came to us, she was barely old enough to leave her mother, she's under the delusion that I'm Mom. And she seems to think my son, all six feet of him, is her kitten; and when she's in her motherly cycle, she chases after him with short insistent mews, wanting him to follow her.

Most of the time, she follows me around like a clingy toddler. Who needs an alarm clock? In the morning she leaps on me, purring, waking me up. She rests on my chest, making it hard to get up when she feels like a living hot water bottle. When I pick out my clothes, she hops into the drawers. She nestles in and seems insulted when I evict her with a plop. When I pray, she curls on the back of my neck, purring in time to my prayers.

At times I find myself trying to do chores with her practically wrapped around my ankles. As I prepare meals, she looks at me longingly, daring me to resist her soulful green eyes, her little wiggling nose, her pink, flicking tongue. She particularly likes to beg chocolate milk from my son.

As I write, she tries her paw at typing, walking across the keys, batting away at the cursor, writing in an unknown language.

We dubbed her Psycho-kitty. She runs up and down the hallway, sounding like a galloping horse, and even at times climbs straight up the walls to the ceiling. When something shiny like a CD reflects on the wall or furniture, she stands on her hind legs, like a meerkat scouting out the African plains, then she chases after the reflection with a peculiar chirping sound.

In the evening, as I read, she sits on the book, bumping my glasses with her nose, declaring herself more important than that inanimate bunch of words on pages. When I do floor exercises, she bats and nips at my fingers. She seems to be indignant that I dare invade her space, though she has no qualms about invading mine.

At times, God's people behave toward God like cats behave toward their owners, wanting His provisions, His comforts, His help in our own terms and timing. But when He reaches down into our business, we bat and nip at His fingers.

He is our provider, our help, our healer; but He does not exist for our pleasure, we exist for His. So as we draw near to Him and He draws near to us; let us welcome His presence, even if at times we may feel He, in His holiness, invades our space.

WATCH-CAT ON THE PROWL

CHERYL ELAINE WILLIAMS

This is what the Lord says to me: "Go, post a lookout and have him report what he sees."... And the lookout shouted, "Day after day, my lord, I stand on the watchtower; every night I stay at my post."

ISAIAH 21:6, 8 NIV

"Settle down, Whiskers. You're excitable today, boy." I frowned as I looked up from my book. Why couldn't my black tabby settle down and give me some peace?

Meow! No rest for the weary today. Whiskers jumped up onto the windowsill overlooking the back patio. He began pacing back and forth on the ledge with his eyes focused intently on something outside.

"What is it, boy? What do you see?" I got up from my armchair. "Is Chippy out there?" Whiskers loved to chase that hated chipmunk. "Squirrely squirrel?" Ditto for the squirrels that scampered down to steal seed from our bird feeders. Their commotion chased away the sweet little birds. That's when I'd open the door and let Whiskers bound outside after them. However, I always checked before I opened that door. It could be something with a stripe.

Hiss! Whiskers pawed the glass. My baby was desperate to pounce.

"Okay, let's see what's out there." I stepped onto my patio and came face-to-face with a lone doe. She was busy chewing the leaves of my tomato plants. I jumped; she jumped, a foot in the air, then landed before freezing. She stared at me, I stared back.

Broad daylight, no less. The deer were getting bold as summer turned into autumn. Food was less plentiful. But I'd nursed those tomato plants all summer and naturally wanted the harvest for my own family, not hers.

"Hey! Get out of here. Shoo." I stomped my foot. The doe darted backward as I took several steps forward. Then she hesitated, retreating no farther. She gazed at me with her nose twitching, taking in my scent. Her attitude was, is there some mistake?

No mistake, pal. "Yes, I mean you. Keep your nose out of my plants. Piglet!"

She wasn't intimidated one bit. I reached for a hoe that I'd left upright by the chimney. "Go, git." The implement in my grasp got her attention, and she bolted. Over the hill toward the industrial park area of my neighborhood where there were woods. Back through the opening in the fence she'd come through.

I inspected my plants. She'd cleaned off the two end vines from which several big tomatoes I'd been watching were now absent. *Grrr!*

I should've picked them yesterday, I knew. I'd gotten greedy, letting them get bigger and bigger just to see how large they could get. Now it was too late. However, my visitor had left me a number of medium-size tomatoes.

"Thanks to you, Whiskers," I told my watch-cat. I let Whiskers outside so he could prance about his patio. He "helped" me pick the bigger tomatoes that were left. "Good baby," I complimented him. "You helped save Mommy's garden."

We went inside and I grilled cheese and tomato sandwiches for lunch. Whiskers took a few bites as his treat. He earned it, my faithful guardian. After this, I stopped complaining when my tabby fussed at the windowsill. Like the watchman in the Bible, he was content to be at his post.

THE CAT'S MEOW:
LOVE

The reasons we share our lives with our cats may be different, and yet somehow they are tied by a common thread. It is love that links us together: love of the animals and their love for us, for reasons known only to them, but it's all the same. It's all love.

SARA WILSON

WHEN. . .it's AMORE (LOVE)

Dee Aspin

We love him, because he first loved us.

1 John 4:19 KJV

One morning when my brother was five, my parents received a call from Cipriani School. "Michael is sitting here in our principal's office elated. He has a cat in his lap."

Michael had always loved cats. One day, after a trip to the grocery store with Dad, he came home with George—apparently an uncouth alley cat. My mom branded George immediately, "*not a good cat.*"

He loved to claw and scratch the screens on the windows—with terrible screeching sounds. Mom, my little brother, and I were afraid of George. The neighbors offered to take him off Mom's hands since Dad was gone a lot. But Michael loved George. Every night he slept with him and he fed him faithfully.

Michael also loved his first-grade teacher, Mrs. Curtis. Although she was immensely pregnant, he had a huge crush on her. Mom soon noticed that Michael walked daily up our hilly street to sit on the corner curb of Cipriani Avenue after school. He patiently waited for his teacher to drive by his spot. When she passed her starstruck student, she smiled as he grinned and passionately waved good-bye.

One day George disappeared. Michael was heartbroken. Frantic, he and his dad searched the neighborhood and spoke to anyone they could find. Michael was very upset and at night he prayed God would help him find his cat.

One week after George left, Michael was sitting in class, listening attentively to his beloved teacher when the class broke out in laughter. Startled, Mrs. Curtis stopped reading her story and looked down. Michael immediately recognized the familiar figure rubbing back and forth affectionately against Mrs. Curtis's legs.

"That's my cat!" he screamed in excitement as the other children rejoiced with him.

Mom was not surprised when she received the call from school where George had reappeared that morning. She said he had developed the same ardor for Mrs. Curtis that my brother, his owner, had.

Throughout the Bible there is a continual theme of God loving His people and seeking after them even when they reject Him and are doing bad things. God always gives them opportunity to change and return home to Him whenever they have wandered off.

If we pray to God and read His Word, it is impossible not to know Him. If we know Him, we will love the things He loves and is excited about. He is excited about His creatures.

If we have a difficult time loving certain people in our world, the best thing we can do is pray for them. This is why Jesus said to pray for our enemies.

God sees the reasons they have bad behavior. He knows their past and where they came from. He knows the hurts that cause them to hurt those around them. Hurt people, hurt people—attack cats have probably been attacked.

Just as Michael embraced George and saw the love he was capable of giving, we never need doubt that if we commit difficult people to God, He will reveal their loving side sooner or later . . .and we may even be part of the solution.

CAN A CAT LOVE A DOG?

CHRISTENA STRUBEN

If anyone says, "I love God," yet hates his brother, he is a liar.
For anyone who does not love his brother, whom he has seen, cannot
love God, whom he has not seen. And he has given us this command:
Whoever loves God must also love his brother.

1 JOHN 4:20–21 NIV

While visiting the small historic town of Harper's Ferry, Virginia, we found a tiny kitten under our car. His cry was heart wrenching. He appeared too small to be separated from his mother. Hotel staff admitted that the little beggar had been hanging around for several days, looking for handouts. It seemed that no one wanted him. We scooped him up and took him to a veterinarian who found him to be full of fleas and too thin, but generally healthy. The vet explained to us that Harper's Ferry was overrun with feral cats. Most likely there would be no home for him in this town. So, of course, we took him with us.

We named him Harper, and he meowed his way into our hearts before we pulled into the driveway at home. Job number one was to familiarize Harper with the pet waiting for us behind the front door. Faith, our black Labrador retriever, was the present "master of the house." Sweet, gentle, patient Faith was used to being the center of our attention. How would she handle this tiny intruder whom she could swallow in one bite if she wanted to?

Slowly, we introduced Harper to Faith. The only problem we encountered was that Faith loved her new roommate too much. She could knock him over with one overzealous lick. As Harper grew, the relationship became one resembling that of siblings. Now, they give each other an occasionally friendly smack and Harper piles on top of Faith for a warm nap.

Harper, however, has a bit more spunk than Faith. His special joy is to tease his canine "sibling." We keep small dog biscuits in a bowl on a dresser to reward Faith for certain behaviors. The treats are too high for Faith to reach. But Harper is able to jump up and take control of the dog snacks. He does not want them for himself; he wants to use them to "torture" Faith. He dips his paw into the bowl, takes out one biscuit at a time, and nudges it to the edge. Pretty soon, Faith's full attention is on Harper and the bowl of treats. The biscuit teeters on the edge of the dresser. Faith barks. Harper pretends to ignore her. He will not push the biscuit over to Faith's waiting mouth, until the dog sits and begs with her eyes. This activity is repeated until the bowl is empty. Harper loves it, Faith loves it, and we love to watch it.

Harper and Faith have a sweet loving relationship—like siblings.

God receives us as His beloved. He calls on us to love Him, but also to love one another. It is the intent of the heavenly Father that we act as siblings: loving, giving, forgiving, and sharing. We honor Him and all He has done for us by following His commandments. Because His love dwells in us we are able to have sweet loving relationships with our brothers and sisters in Christ.

A TALE ABOUT TAILS

MARCIA HORNOK

His compassions never fail. They are new every morning;
great is your faithfulness.

LAMENTATIONS 3:22–23 NIV

In Hawaii, Cindy's varicolored cat named Kate loved to go to the beach. She would swat at the waves when they washed up to where she stood and pat the bubbles left behind. She liked to dig in the sand with both front paws, looking for hermit crabs.

Another thing about Hawaii that Kate loved were the geckos that clung to walls inside the house. But Kate had the unfortunate habit of biting their tails off. A gecko's tail grows back, but guests in Cindy's home would see a tailless gecko and ask what happened.

"We have a cat," Cindy would tell them. That explained it.

Although Kate tormented geckos, she had a gentle, affectionate nature. When she rubbed against someone's leg, Cindy called it a "cat-hug." Whenever someone reached down to pet her soft fur, Kate would roll on her back like a dog to have her tummy stroked.

These favorite things made Kate unique. When Cindy moved to Utah, however, Kate no longer had the beach or geckos to play with. No more ocean waves to swat back or crabs to find. And no more tails to taste. Everything had changed. Except her owner's love. Kate still had Cindy taking care of all her needs, holding and petting her, talking to her, and scratching her head.

Sometimes life throws major changes our way. We lose things we love and have to go on living without them. Many times an unexpected event forces us to give up places or people we enjoyed. Our losses may be permanent, but so is God's love.

The older we get, the more changes we have to adjust to, but one thing will never change—the steadfast love of God. The hymn "Be Still My Soul" states: "In every change He faithful will remain."

I don't think Kate misses gecko tails so much. Not when she has Cindy to stroke her belly every day.

GOING WHERE tHE CAt iS

RACHEL QUILLIN

*And when the Pharisees saw it, they said unto his disciples,
Why eateth your Master with publicans and sinners?*

MATTHEW 9:11 KJV

When our first three children were small we noticed that they were quite drawn to the cats on the farm, and we began to discuss the possibility of bringing a kitten to the house as a pet. So when our nice mama cat weaned a batch of kittens, my husband selected one and brought her home. The kids were thrilled and promptly named her Mingo.

Personally I have always liked cats, but with three young kids and plans for more, I couldn't see the wisdom in making this an indoor cat. Plus part of the purpose of the kitten was to keep the mice at bay. However, she was not completely tame at this point, and we were afraid she would return to her family before the kids had the opportunity to love her into submission. That is why my husband decided to use a large animal cage for a short while. We made sure the kids understood that Mingo was to be in the cage when they weren't playing with her. We warned them that she might run off if they weren't careful.

They took our admonition seriously. Very seriously. One afternoon, shortly after Mingo's arrival, I was doing some housework. The baby was asleep, and my son was spending time on the tractor with Daddy. I noticed that my daughter Moriah was being very quiet. That is always cause for alarm as she is not known for being quiet—even while she sleeps. I began my investigation and soon discovered her whereabouts. She had locked herself inside the cage with her new little buddy, and they were spending quality time together.

Many different things ran through my mind at that moment. Even while laughing, I was wondering how Moriah had managed such a feat. Being our little Houdini I'm sure she would have just as easily made her escape when she was ready. I also remember very distinctly thinking how gross it was that my beautiful two-year-old child was inside a cage with a cat.

She had no qualms about it herself. For a small child she had a very large vocabulary, and she let me know in no uncertain terms that she wanted to play with Mingo, but she didn't want Mingo to run away, so she thought it would be best to spend the afternoon in the cat's cage. What was I to do besides laugh and grab the camera?

Unfortunately as Christians, we're not always quite so understanding. We're quick to pass judgment on those who would reach out to the "unlovelies" of this world. All too often we take on the form of "Christian" snobbery, and we expect other Christians to do the same. In that, we're no better than the Pharisees.

Moriah was more like Jesus. She wanted to influence her kitten just like Jesus wanted to affect the lost. He didn't participate in their sins, but He knew that in order to reach them He would need to show them love and compassion. He commissioned us to do the same. It's time we followed His lead.

A Life of Gratitude

JO UPTON

Give thanks to the LORD and proclaim his greatness.
Let the whole world know what he has done.

1 Chronicles 16:8 NLT

Living on two acres of wooded property, we were accustomed to animal sounds. But one day, after listening for only a few seconds, we realized what we were hearing didn't fall into the "normal" category. It sounded more like the screams of something small and without hope.

A quick survey of the front yard revealed a beautiful gray kitten with long hair, stubby legs, and small pointed ears. He looked more like a baby owl than anything in the feline family. We went toward him, expecting him to run, but instead he just sat there. We bundled him in a towel, for his warmth and our safety, and took him to a nearby vet.

An examination revealed that this very young kitten was dehydrated, nearly starved, and apparently close to death. His wailing had been a last-minute cry for help. The doctor hooked him to various tubes, but warned us that he couldn't guarantee anything. We left wondering if he would make it through the night.

The next day we were told that the kitten was eating and seemed stronger. Realizing this had probably taken several of his nine lives, we decided to bring him home and nurse him back to health. Thus began our relationship with this large-eyed kitten that looked like something that had fallen to earth from a nest in the trees. We called him Hooty.

At first, Hooty wasn't sure he could trust us. He would scurry from spot to spot, hiding under furniture to watch our activities from a safe distance. But after a few weeks of care, and probably a hundred bowls of kitten food, he began to respond with love... *lots* of love.

I don't think I've ever had a cat show as much affection as Hooty. He attached himself to me and became my shadow. In the beginning it was probably for food, but soon things changed. If I went to a room without him, he would cry softly until I answered and he found me. When I sat down, he would sit on the floor at my feet, try to make eye contact, then wait for me to motion him into my lap. Once there, he would continue to climb until he reached my face and then gently pat my cheeks with his paws. He was totally devoted. His actions implied that he realized, somehow fully understood, that he would have perished had someone not heard his cry.

God heard our cry. Through Jesus, He has shown us how deeply He loves us and His plan for our salvation. It's more than we can comprehend, and it's something we never deserved. Our gratitude and thankfulness should overflow, making it impossible for us to remain quiet. God has provided hope and healing for a hurting world—let's tell somebody!

RESCUING tHE PERISHING CAt

MEREDITH LEBLANC

So, as those who have been chosen of God, holy and beloved, put on a heart of compassion, kindness, humility, gentleness and patience.

COLOSSIANS 3:12 NASB

Clearwater, Florida—hot and muggy, with a threat of thunderstorms—was an unfriendly place for a solid black, stray cat lurking on the beach behind the restaurant next to our condo. The poor creature was desperate for food and fresh water. My son, David, knew as soon as he spotted the feline in need, he must rescue this pitiful ball of fur.

David rushed to the condo to find a can of tuna and bowls for food and water. Then he returned to the beach, praying to find the cat still there. He was so thankful when he spied him digging around a trash bin, searching desperately for food. In David's mind he had already named him Buster. Patience and compassion were needed to coax Buster to trust him. Eventually David got close enough to catch the cat—but not without much feline clawing, hissing, and fighting. As they entered the condo, Buster rushed to the window and climbed the drapes. The only recourse was to lock him in the bathroom while David prepared a bed and safe place for him.

But Buster would not be tamed without loads of loving kindness. When anyone came to the door, there were howls of protest. Upon receiving guests, he climbed David's leg, leaving claw marks before reaching his shorts. His exploits included hiding in a storage bin on the balcony for days before we could locate him, ravished and thirsty; and hiding under the bed, unwilling to come out even with the enticement of delicious treats. One afternoon Buster escaped, tearing down the hall in search of a way out. Just like the gingerbread man he seemed to call "run, run as fast as you can, you can't catch me. . . ." At the end of the hall and at a bank of unopened elevators, with David and two other neighbors catching up to him, Buster was once again rescued.

Buster's first trip to the veterinarian is legendary in that office. Now when it's time for Buster to visit the vet, he is given what amounts to valium for cats. The vet and his assistant don protective gloves that cover to the elbow. Then—and only then—are they ready to examine Buster.

You might wonder if this cat was worth rescuing. He has been a reluctant captive at best. David bears the marks of Buster's defiant ways. There is no accounting for the boy's love of the cat. With determination, however, David captured Buster's heart. Now there is a mutual love and respect between the cat and the boy. Buster has come to realize he has been rescued.

God's love for us, sinful, defiant creatures, is infinite. He pursues us for a love relationship. He rescues us from the pit of hell for a future with Him, now and for eternity. Just like Buster, we are thankful to be rescued.

CONFESSIONS OF A FORMER CAT HATER

GLENN A. HASCALL

God demonstrates his own love for us in this:
While we were still sinners, Christ died for us.

ROMANS 5:8 NIV

They say confession is good for the soul. There is no other way to say this—I hate cats. Well, that is until four years ago when I met Sassy. She was a neighbor's cat that felt she was the neighborhood Welcome Wagon. She dropped by to say hello when we moved to town and, for some reason, she adopted us.

Sass is a patchwork-quilt cat, a calico with attitude. To prove her loyalty, she would often leave birds and mice on our front step. Sass had two offspring and a sister. They would often join her in her visits to our home, but it didn't take long for Sass to send them away. We were her family, and there would be no breach of familial etiquette.

There is a special bond between my daughter and Sass. I often watch the two through the front window. My daughter will open her arms wide, and Sass will crouch and jump into her arms immediately flopping on her back to be held in much the same way a mother might hold her young. Her eyes close and her claws stretch, her inner purr mechanism sounds like a chainsaw; and for a moment, there is no place so wonderful in the universe than my daughter's arms for that cat.

I love that cat. There, I said it. I do.

Do I love Sass because I experienced a Scrooge-type revelation when I have seen the error of my ways and lament the years devoid of feline affection? Not really. I love that cat for the unconditional love she has shown my family. I love the cat because she chose us to love. Sass didn't ask my permission to show love—she just demonstrated love and waited for me to soften. I did.

Isn't that just like God? He showed love when He didn't have to. He kept knocking even when we kept the door to our inner lives tightly shut and pretended the knocking was something else entirely. And while He knocked, He jealously protected us from dangers we never knew about. He just kept loving us.

He kept leaving us amazing life gifts including sunshine, rain, air, and food. He kept showing up with blessings in so many shapes and sizes, yet we kept thinking of them as coincidences or the product of our own labor. He kept loving us.

And in that moment when we finally came to the place where we could admit a love for the God who made us, we experienced a love for the God who lavished so much attention on us, and finally caught a glimpse of how crazy God is for us. He just kept on loving us.

What's even more amazing is that we can find incredible joy in the God who makes a difference in the lives of others. We can actually be overwhelmingly giddy that God is big enough to adopt others into His family.

WHY FRISKY OUTSANG tHE CHOIR

CONNIE PETERS

*How great is the love the Father has lavished on us, that we
should be called children of God! And that is what we are!*

1 JOHN 3:1 NIV

While my children and I sat in church one Sunday morning, our cat sat outside on the window ledge and wailed louder than the choir. I commissioned my ten-year-old son to capture her and take her across the yard to our mobile home on the church property. It wasn't till after church that we realized the reason for the concert. Frisky (don't blame me, my daughter named her) had had her kittens and apparently forgotten where she put them. Each time she crawled into a box, bag, or behind the couch, we thought, *Eureka!* but nothing.

That night, when I tucked my two children into bed, they asked about the baby kittens. Would they be okay?

As a busy mom I've been absentminded at times, but I never

forgot where I put my children. "Mama Cat will find where she put her kittens," I reassured them, hoping I was right. We'd been having warm spring days, but it was still a bit nippy at night.

At last, I sat down in the kitchen with a hot cup of tea, glad to have a quiet moment. And then I heard them. So much for the quiet moment.

In my pj's and slippers, like a cat burglar, I tiptoed outside around our trailer with a flashlight and promptly dismantled part of the skirting. Shivering, I hunkered down and peeked underneath, with images of spiders and snakes dancing in my head. "Come out, come out, wherever you are." I was answered by some desperate mewing above my head.

I'm sure Frisky meant well when she hid her kitties between the floorboards and insulation. I fetched a knife from the kitchen, hoping that my neighbors wouldn't be watching and worrying from their windows. I crawled back into the trailer's underbelly and carefully cut through the black plastic. I pulled out two adorable kittens crying for all they were worth, one tiger striped, the other, looking very Halloween-ish, black with orange dots.

When I brought them inside and made a soft place for them in the bathroom, their mews brought Mama Cat and both children running. Maybe because it was like the kitties had been lost in space, my kids named them after Star Trek characters, Geordi and Data.

I marveled at how I felt about those two noisy bits of fluff, both of which could easily fit inside my teacup. I felt as if I'd acted as midwife and delivered those kittens myself. But even more marvelous is how much God loves us frail humans. I left the comforts of home and crawled under a trailer in the cold blackness and stuck my hand up into the unknown. How much more intense and passionate is His love for us, for Jesus to leave heaven and come to earth to deliver us!

LULLABIES AND LOVE SONGS

DARLENE FRANKLIN

"The LORD your God is with you, he is mighty to save.
He will take great delight in you, he will quiet you with his love,
he will rejoice over you with singing."

ZEPHANIAH 3:17 NIV

When I was in high school, I practiced my clarinet every day. I was good—really, I was. I even made first clarinet in the all-state band. . .so don't assume anything based on my cat Mike's behavior.

Whenever I sat down and began to blow, Mike jumped on my lap. He rubbed against my fingers, making it impossible for me to play. When I did manage to extricate my digits from his rubbing, he "sang" right along with my clarinet. But if I wanted to get any serious practice time in, Mike had to go outside.

Fortunately, Talia, the cat who currently claims me as her human, feels differently about my music. (The fact I'm not playing a clarinet might help.)

I'm the prototypical songbird in the shower. Get me under hot water, and music flows out of me. When I'm bored, I sing.

"Ninety-nine splashes of water to go, ninety-nine splashes to go. . . ." I generally make it out of the bath with about "forty" to spare, and continue singing to see if I can finish dressing before I run out of splashes.

Talia's favorite time to spend with me is when I'm getting dressed. She casually approaches the door to my room and lies down so that only her seal-point ears or tail can be seen.

I woo her into the room. "Twenty-five splashes of water to go. . .Talia, Talia, twenty-four splashes to go."

At the sound of her name, Talia's ears bend forward. By the time I've repeated it two or three times, she has abandoned her carefree posture and joined me at my feet, meowing at every mention of her name.

Other mornings I sing different melodies, but all with the same lyrics: Tal-e-a, three syllables, or Tal-ya, two syllables, depending on the rhythm. One of our favorites is the nursery rhyme "Pussy Cat, Pussy Cat, Where Have You Been?" "Talia" substitutes perfectly for "pussy cat." She's been to London hundreds of times—at least in song.

Other times I croon in a singsong voice, "Talia, she is a girl. Talia, she is a pearl. Talia, she has no curls." When she meows, I agree, "I know, cats don't have curls."

Sometimes we continue playing the game throughout the day, when I'm sitting at the computer or unpacking a box. When she hears her name, she takes it as an invitation to join me wherever I am.

I sing to Talia because she is precious to me and because I love it when she knows I'm talking to her.

Zephaniah says God feels the same way about us. God quiets us with His love; He rejoices over us with singing.

Like a father singing a lullaby to his baby.

Or like me singing to my cat.

KRiNGLe tHE CHRiStMAS KittY

DEBRA ANN ELLIOTT

Thanks be to God for his indescribable gift!

2 CORINTHIANS 9:15 NIV

It was the end of November, and Christmas was fast approaching. My grandson was excited. He couldn't wait until Santa's visit. About two weeks before Christmas, he started making out his Christmas list.

"Cameron, what did you ask Santa to bring you for Christmas?"

"A kitty, Nana." *A kitty?* We already had two cats, and my husband wasn't about to add to our extended family. Samson and Delilah ruled the roost; bringing another kitty into the mix spelled trouble.

"A kitty? You want Santa to bring you a *real* kitty?"

"Yup! I want a kitty just like my friend." I wasn't sure how to explain Santa may not be able to bring him a real kitty.

"We'll have to wait until Christmas and see what Santa brings you, okay?"

"*Please*, Nana, ask Santa to bring me a kitty for Christmas!" I tucked him in, kissed him, and let him know I'd put in a good word with Santa. I already knew what "Santa" would say. *No way!*

I walked into the den where my husband was reading the newspaper. "Honey, Cameron wants Santa to bring him a kitty for Christmas." I waited for Dave's reaction.

"A kitty?"

"Yup, a real kitty, he informed me."

"Annie, you know we can't get another cat."

"I know, but can we go to the shelter and look around?"

"I guess, but no promises."

It was a done deal! I knew once Dave got to the shelter, we would come home with a kitty for Christmas. We waited until Christmas Eve to go to our local shelter. If there was a kitten we liked, I knew it would come home with us.

The shelter worker greeted us. "May I help you?"

No, I wanted to say. "Yes, we're looking for a kitten for our grandson."

She took us to the back where several metal cages lined the walls. Cats of all colors and sizes decorated the pens. I passed several cages before I saw the indescribably adorable white kitten curled up into a tight ball. I knew we had found our Christmas kitty! The worker removed the kitten from its cage and handed it to me. The little white powder puff instantly started purring.

"Well?" I looked at Dave.

"Alright, we'll get Cameron his Christmas kitty." We weren't sure how our *other* two cats would react, but this little guy was going home with us! Dave paid the shelter fees, and we took our new "baby" home.

"What are we going to call him?"

I looked at the kitten asleep in my lap. "I don't know. What about Cotton?"

Dave shook his head. "What about Kringle?"

"*Kringle?*"

"Yes, as in Kris Kringle."

"Kringle the Christmas kitty it is then!"

There are many indescribably wonderful gifts like Kringle we receive every day, not only at Christmas. But the most important indescribable gift *we can* receive is the gift of God's love.

ALL IN IT TOGETHER

BETTY OST-EVERLEY

How good and pleasant it is when
brothers live together in unity!

PSALM 133:1 NIV

When we moved into our house, we found the neighborhood was a feral cat haven. Neither of our elderly dogs appreciated that, barking furiously every time a cat walked past the door. The cats weren't intimidated one bit.

That we were dog owners didn't stop my husband's feline fascination. Three cats "came" with the house, two nearly identical orange marmalade tabby males and a solid black female. They frequently slept in the window well outside our downstairs bathroom, and he would talk to them through the window. They became known by the very original names of Frick, Frack, and Blackie.

"Look, honey, Frick now lets me pet him. I'm sure it was because we bonded as males when I spoke to him through the window," my husband exclaimed.

Male bonding? I wasn't ready to accept *that* as the reason, but I was amazed that Frick allowed us to touch him. Eventually, we could hold and hand-feed him.

Over the next year, Frack left for parts unknown. Blackie was never as friendly as Frick, but they did enjoy being fed together on the back porch. When both dogs had to be put down because of failing health, Frick was finally allowed to come into the house. Glory! He realized inside was a much nicer place to hang out than a window well. Our home became his castle! Instead of sleeping underneath a tree, he adopted our couch. He especially loved sitting on our laps and even sometimes slept with us.

Blackie's life also changed when she became a mother the next spring. It was obvious Frick couldn't have fathered the kittens since two were jet-black like Blackie and the other two were black and white tuxedos. Frick didn't seem to mind them. He acted somewhat like a big brother, teaching the youngsters to chase and hunt. The kittens also taught Frick something—how to play. He evidently never learned that, and it was delightful to see a big cat beside little ones wrestling a stick.

When winter approached, we felt the kittens we had successfully socialized needed a safe place to live, and not in the window well. A family member and a neighbor took a tuxedo each. Solid black cats are sometimes difficult to place, so we took the other two.

We went from a two-dog to a three-cat household. There were times when I wasn't sure it was the right thing to do, having three cats share the same space, especially when they were used to wide open spaces. Over time, they did learn to get along and respect each other, sometimes even grooming each other.

Father God expects much the same of His children. Each of

us comes from different environments and experiences. Yet, He wants us to live together in unity, accepting our differences, loving and respecting each other. Jesus gives us many tools, forgiveness being one of them. Paul says we should get along as well as we can. Commit today to live in unity!

WE HAVE THIS CAT

GAYLE LINTZ

For he chose us in him before the creation of the world to be holy and blameless in his sight. In love he predestined us to be adopted as his sons through Jesus Christ, in accordance with his pleasure and will—to the praise of his glorious grace, which he has freely given us in the One he loves.

EPHESIANS 1:4–6 NIV

Here's how it happened.

My wife came home one day from the dance studio where she teaches. A cat had turned up there, apparently alone and homeless. The studio owner couldn't keep it but was hoping to find it a loving, permanent home. Meanwhile, she was looking for temporary lodging for the cat. Softhearted Sarah said we could keep it for a few days and brought it home.

Now, I can hear all of you snickering as you read this. You know *exactly* what followed. After Sarah brought the cat to our apartment, the studio owner spent about an hour and a half really trying to find someone who would adopt the vagabond. Then, "Find home for cat" dropped further and further down her "urgent" to-do list, and, within days, we had ourselves a pet.

Our T-Tat didn't look like a homeless, wild feline. She was clean and seemed well-fed. We thought her owners must have had to move from Brooklyn, were unable to take her along, and left her, hoping that some kind cat lover would find her and take her in. It's common here in New York for people to put things they no longer want or need out on the curb for anyone to claim. We ourselves have picked up shelves, a desk, and books off the street. Now, we had found a new family member that way, too.

Neither one of us had ever owned a cat. As a kid, I'd had rabbits as pets, and my brother had gerbils. Sarah's family owned a couple of dogs, years before. Thank heaven for the Internet. We researched cat owner sites and learned that T-Tat is an American shorthaired cat. We read that dry food is as healthy as canned food. Cats need a place to scratch. They can be trained to use the toilet.

When I walked through the living room with a bottle of window cleaner and she bolted, we assumed that at some point she'd been trained with a spray bottle. We discovered that when she lies down on her back, with her paws in the air, it does *not* mean that she wants her tummy rubbed. She went to the nearby vet's for shots and spaying. Sarah's mother and my aunt bought her gifts for Christmas. My mother gave us a special brush to whisk away animal hair.

T-Tat became a full-fledged member of the family, and all she had to do was show up.

We don't have to do even that much to be adopted into the family of God. He loved us *before* we showed up. He did love us. He does love us. He will love us. Thank heaven.

CURIOSITY KILLED THE CAT: TRUSTING GOD

Watch a cat when it enters a room for the first time.
It searches and smells about, it is not quiet for a moment,
it trusts nothing until it has examined and made
acquaintance with everything.

JEAN-JACQUES ROUSSEAU

IN tHE PINK

DARLENE FRANKLIN

*"You will nurse and be carried on her arm and dandled on her knees.
As a mother comforts her child, so will I comfort you."*

ISAIAH 66:12–13 NIV

My son's family cat, Pinkie, is a study in contradictions, starting with his name. Whoever heard of naming a black tomcat with a tiny white stripe under chin and belly *Pinkie?* When I asked his owner, my granddaughter Shannon, she said, "We didn't know he was a boy when we named him." I wouldn't have named a mainly black cat of either gender "Pinkie," but perhaps the image of a tiny tongue flicking around his bewhiskered face inspired Shannon's childish thinking.

In addition to the contradiction between color and name, "Pinkie" suggests a small cat, like a little finger. Instead, he looks huge—especially with his fluffy long hair. When he states "meow" in his insistent, high-pitched voice, I pay attention and let him in (or out) of the door—or get his dinner pronto.

In spite of his tough tomcat exterior, Pinkie's a big softie inside. He always befriends me, an occasional guest in his house. One day Shannon told me, "You can have Pinkie, if you like."

I explained the facts of life to Shannon. My Talia prefers her solitary existence. Besides, I'd have to pay a big deposit for a second pet.

In spite of my objections, Pinkie must have approved of Shannon's idea. When I prepared to leave, I found him waiting on the roof of my car. (If he wanted warmth from the engine, wouldn't he have chosen the hood?) He blinked his yellow eyes at me as if to say, "I'm ready to leave." The next time I visited, he climbed back on the roof as if determined to make his home with me.

Even though I didn't adopt Pinkie, he still allows me to be his friend. When the house is quiet and the baby asleep, Pinkie indulges in one of his favorite pastimes. He climbs onto my lap and settles in for a nice long cuddle. He starts out *in* my lap, but soon creeps up my chest, places his front paws on my shoulders, and begins licking my ear and kneading my skin.

My son theorizes that Pinkie was weaned too young. When he finds an accommodating human, he pretends he's a baby again. Instead of being a grown tom, he imagines he's a helpless kitten enjoying the comfort of his mother's protection.

Like Pinkie, at times we wish we could curl up in our mothers' laps and let them comfort us. As adults, we have long since outgrown that recourse. But regardless of our age, we can always go to God as a child seeks out her parent; and He will take us in His arms and comfort us.

Snowball Express

Dee Aspin

He is my loving God and my fortress, my stronghold and my deliverer, my shield, in whom I take refuge.

Psalm 144:2 NIV

Marie had a gorgeous long-haired albino cat with a flat pink nose. Daily her puffball tore rapidly up and down the hallway at the speed-of-white—earning the name Snowball Express. Each sprint ended with a precision dive under Marie's queen bed, braking suddenly, strategically positioned. Safe from the reach of human intruders, he squatted perfectly centered under the mattress. Snowball Express seemed to purr with pride after his exercise routine. He hunkered down happy for the day, always a step ahead of his owners—or so it seemed.

Unknown to her cat, one day Marie's mom lent the bed to the pastor of their church. He carted it off in the evening. The following morning at the appointed time, Snowball Express raced down the hallway to his favorite sanctuary. He made a dive, then assumed camouflage position—only to discover his cover was gone.

He slowly looked to the left, then to the right as he realized his whole body was exposed. Not only was the mattress gone, but the frame. Probably feeling the ventilation, he inched his head up and gazed at Marie—standing above him, grinning. His face contorted in horror, his kitty jaw dropped, and his eyes grew as big as saucers. He squatted under—nothing—only empty space all around him and the ceiling of the room useless at ten feet above his head.

He had dived under an imaginary bed! What he thought was an impregnable fortress turned into a fairy-tale castle. Now his pursuer could exert force over his poor little furry body. Escaping the laughter and humiliation of discovery and defeat, Snowball Express frowned and skittered off past Marie and back down the hall as fast and far away as possible.

What do we try to hide behind that is only a temporary refuge? We place our trust in our jobs for provision—jobs that can end as the seasons turn. We depend on our farms to provide crops for food, while the farmer looks to the weather report for success.

Who brings the rain? Who is over the storm?

We look around us and nothing there represents stability and true safety. But Jesus spoke of a heavenly Father who feeds the sparrows even though they are not able to reap or sow or store away in barns. And He assures us, we are more valuable than the sparrows.

Invest in heaven, store your treasures above where they cannot be lost or stolen, Jesus taught us. We can all get stuck in a rut of routine and forget, as we race through our days, that everything we have on earth is temporary. How much more valuable to build up eternal rewards that can never be taken away and find true sanctuary in our Creator.

CAtCH it!

KATHERINE DOUGLAS

*Catch for us the foxes, the little foxes that ruin the vineyards,
our vineyards that are in bloom.*

SONG OF SOLOMON 2:15 NIV

"Catch it!"

"What?"

"I don't know! It's brown—or gray—and it's moving fast!"

"I think I see it! No. . .wait. It's only Scarlet's tail. Where did it go, Scarlet?"

"Don't ask her, she can't. . . . *Eeeeeeek*! It's a mouse! Get it!"

"Where is it? Where did it go?"

"The refrigerator—it's behind the refrigerator! Catch it before it gets away!"

And so it goes. Another day in the family life of Scarlet O'Gray, the cat. Scarlet, in her Ohio State University colors of gray fur and red collar, doesn't follow the family's favorite college team like the rest of the family. No football or basketball for Scarlet. Scarlet's game is pursuit.

Scarlet O'Gray enjoys a carefully controlled chase. The world outside makes for too much work. Why pursue outside where her opponent can more easily get away? Scarlet grew up as a stray cat; she knows what a harsh world exists outside her comfy quarters. So she brings the game inside. With her opponent hanging from her mouth, Scarlet pries open the screen door with one paw and carries in her unfortunate quarry. Once inside, she opens her mouth, and drops her prey on the floor.

The race is on! The befuddled animal runs from corner to corner, under furniture and around tables with Scarlet in fun-loving pursuit. Scarlet wouldn't think of killing her victim. She is, after all, well fed and cared for now. Pursuit, like football, is only a game. But Scarlet's game—to Joan's woe—always ends up the same.

After the game is over, Scarlet meanders off to rest. It's up to Joan or someone else in the family to escort the still very fast-moving victim outside again. Joan has had to catch and return mice, moles, chipmunks, and snakes to the outdoors. Joan prefers OSU football to Scarlet O'Gray's cat and quarry game.

In the Song of Solomon, we read about a new bride and her husband. The couple protectively guards its love, but somehow life butts in. Not moles or mice, but marriage stressors Solomon calls "the little foxes."

The things of greatest value in our lives are people and our relationships with them. Whether it's our relationship with the Lord Jesus Christ, our spouse, our family, or our friends, it's far easier to get focused on things that demand our attention. The people who need or want our time aren't often right there saying so. Demands at work, our scheduled appointments, and tasks around the house are the "foxes," both small and big, that distract us. These "foxes," like Scarlet's unwilling playmates, pull us in every direction, leaving people and the forfeited time spent with them in the wake of the chase.

Today the cat might drag in a mouse. A little fox may wreak havoc throughout the vineyard of our most important relationship. May God help us remember what's most important in life's busyness. We'll generally find out it's not a what; it's a who.

Silhouette on the Shape

JANET ROCKEY

"Behold, I stand at the door and knock; if anyone hears My voice and opens the door, I will come in to him and will dine with him, and he with Me."

REVELATION 3:20 NASB

I shared an apartment with my tuxedo cat, Sammy. Aside from not kicking in his share of the rent, he had all the best attributes of a roommate anyone could want. He didn't borrow my clothes, leave dirty dishes in the sink, or take long showers depleting the source of hot water.

He was a faithful fellow, too. I knew when I let him out in the evening, I could trust him to come home before midnight—most of the time.

We had a system worked out. As I lay in bed reading, he announced he was ready to come in, hopefully without a fresh-caught "gift." Not by sitting by the back door and meowing, mind you. Oh no, not dramatic enough for this active kitty. Sammy chose the bedroom window, which had no windowsill for him to hop on to, and body-slammed himself with a loud

THA-FONG!— his silhouette splayed on the window behind the curtain as he clung to the screen.

The back door of the apartment was at the foot of my bed. At his signal, I would crawl over to the foot and open the door. In thirty seconds, he unclenched his claws, dropped to the ground, and trotted inside.

One night, Sammy was later than usual. I was about to open my door to call him, when the familiar *THA-FONG!* pounded not far away. No silhouette appeared on my window. The man in the next apartment yelled, "Wha–? What's that?"

I opened my door. "Sammy!" I whispered. "Over here!"

He unclenched his claws from my neighbor's screen and dropped to the ground, scampering to me. I closed my door as the neighbor opened his.

Unaware, or unconcerned, that he had disturbed the neighbor's sleep, Sammy stretched, washed his face, and hopped up on the bed. He yawned and blinked up at me as I stood breathlessly by the back door. He seemed to say, *Aren't you coming to bed?*

I listened by the door for a moment, but no more sounds came from the neighbor's apartment. I crawled back into the bed, and Sammy curled up next to me. Using my upper arm for his pillow, he purred us both to sleep.

The next day, my neighbor knocked on my door. "Did you hear that noise last night?" he asked.

"Yeah." I offered no explanation and hoped Sammy's aim would improve in the nights to follow. Forget about keeping him in at night. Some battles aren't worth fighting.

I don't know why Sammy went to the wrong window that night. But it's comforting to know that Christ is never at the wrong door. He knows exactly where we are every minute of the day and is ready for us to invite Him in to share His bounty.

MISINTERPRETING
THE EVIDENCE

MARCIA HORNOK

Though he slay me, yet will I trust in him.

JOB 13:15 KJV

When our black cat, Sooty, had a litter, one kitten had multicolored fur, basically gray with streaks of calico. Americans had recently walked on the moon and brought back moon dust, so that's what we named him.

As a kitten, Moondust captured our hearts with his playful antics. He slept with his paw across another kitten. Once when I was packing for a trip, Moondust climbed into my open suitcase and fell asleep, looking exactly like a rolled-up sweater vest. For a while we couldn't find him.

Moondust had one bad habit, however. We thought we had him litter trained until we discovered a puddle by the corner of the fridge. We stuck his nose in it, scolded him, and escorted him to the litter box.

The next day he puddled again in the same place. We used the same procedure, but in the course of a week, nothing had changed.

Suddenly my husband remembered something. "You know last week when the refrigerator bulb burned out?"

"Yes," I replied.

"We didn't have an appliance bulb, so we put in a regular lightbulb. I think heat from that bulb is melting the ice around the freezer section, which makes a puddle on the floor."

Sure enough, Moondust had done nothing wrong. When I tell this story, I usually add, "The poor cat never drank water again," but that's not true. I like to think he forgave and forgot. The problem was not with our cat—it was with our interpretation of the evidence, giving us a faulty view of Moondust.

I have often done this with God. I don't like what He's allowing in my life, and I accuse Him of giving a stone when I asked for bread. The evidence points to His ineffectiveness or unconcern, and I conclude that He must be a mean taskmaster.

Job also knew that feeling. Repeatedly he asked God to defend Himself for the injustices He had allowed Job to experience. Job-like, I also have called God to the courtroom, so to speak.

"Where were You when I needed You most?"

"Why haven't You given me the desires of my heart when doing so would glorify You?"

"How could You not have prevented_____?"

God responded to Job's questions by questioning him—putting him on the witness stand. Job learned that God is not accountable to us. He is too immense and infinite to be figured out. He is perfectly just even though we cannot prove it.

I have learned I don't need to understand God's ways. He is inscrutable to my puny mind. When I don't like the path He has me on, I must resist the urge to misinterpret Him. Like our experience with Moondust, the evidence may indicate a supposed infraction, but God is never wrong. I can always trust Him because of His character and thank Him for His perfect love and wisdom, despite my circumstances.

He knows what He's doing, and that means I don't have to.

PLAYMATES

DARLENE FRANKLIN

When Jesus saw this, he was indignant. He said to them, "Let the little children come to me, and do not hinder them, for the kingdom of God belongs to such as these. I tell you the truth, anyone who will not receive the kingdom of God like a little child will never enter it."

MARK 10:14–15 NIV ·

In the book *Blueberries for Sal*, the toddler Sal encounters a mother bear, and the bear cub meets Sal's mother while both families pick blueberries along the coast of Maine. Robert McCloskey writes, "Sal's mother knew bears, even small bears, were dangerous, and so backed up very slowly." On the other hand, the babies of both species knew no fear—only curiosity.

My granddaughter Jordan and the family's new kitten felt the same way about each other.

The other family pets stayed away from the baby. Muffin, the dog, ran every time Jordan approached. Their adult tomcat teased Jordan, walking by and brushing her face with his fluffy black tail before moving out of reach.

Despite being satisfied that neither adult pet posed a threat to the baby, my son and his wife didn't trust the small kitten adopted into the family. They banished Myster (shortened from Mysterious) to the garage, separated from the main house by a door. Only one problem: The washing machine lay on the kitten's side of the door, and like any cat, Myster *hated* closed doors. As soon as the door opened—which it did on at least a daily basis—he zoomed into the kitchen. And headed straight for Jordan. Because like Sal and the bear cub, the two babies wanted nothing more than to play with each other.

Jordan knew the kitten had soft fur that felt good under her hands. The older cat had taught her that. And unlike almost everyone else in the house, Myster was smaller than she was. Best of all, Myster wanted to play with her. She hadn't yet learned that kittens, even small ones, came equipped with sharp claws that could tear and hurt.

In Jordan, Myster saw someone to take the place of his littermates. She batted her hands and kicked her legs like two kittens wrestling together. He was lonely for the interrupted playtime and so engaged Jordan. He hadn't yet learned that humans, especially babies, could pull, tug, and drop him in ways that hurt.

In spite of the restrictions that Jordan's family put in place to keep kitten and baby separated, they found each other time and again. Much the same thing happened in the passage in Mark. The disciples told parents with small children to go away.

Indignant, Jesus took the children in His lap. He said that only those who come to God as a little child—with the wholehearted joy, curiosity, and trust of Jordan and Myster—will enter His kingdom.

Biting the Hand that Feeds You

MARCIA HORNOK

[Jesus said,] "O Jerusalem, Jerusalem. . . How often I wanted to gather your children together. . .but you were not willing!"

MATTHEW 23:37 NKJV

Steve liked to refer to his multicolored long-haired cat as a brute, because that was the opposite of the cat's nature. The gentle pet had blue eyes and gray, brown, and white fur. Although she was a female, Steve named her Spike.

On the morning of Steve's wedding day, he was in his front yard with Spike at his feet. Two big dogs came running down the sidewalk toward them. Knowing this would freak out Spike, Steve bent over to pick her up and protect her. His touch, however, startled the nervous cat. Spike must have thought she was being attacked and responded in kind.

With claws at full alert, Spike ripped up her owner's hand

with deep cuts, not scratches. Steve attended his wedding ceremony that evening with his right hand and wrist completely bandaged!

Because fear had distorted Spike's thinking, she had attacked her caregiver. I'm afraid I've done that with my Divine Caregiver. Despite His faithful love and provision, when life gets rough, my first instinct is to turn on Him.

Why won't You do something? I don't deserve this. How can You love me and let me suffer this way? It's not fair. I have even accused God of being mean. Looking back, if I had not misinterpreted Him, I would have known He was reaching out to hug me not hurt me.

Life is fearsome at times, but God is not a hard taskmaster who feeds us to the dogs. He knows what He's about. The difficulties He allows will produce a "harvest of righteousness and peace" (Hebrews 12:11 NIV) when I submit to His training process.

Even when circumstances terrify me, I need to trust God's wisdom and keep my claws in.

KNOCKING AT HEAVEN'S DOOR

BETTY OST-EVERLEY

"Ask and it will be given to you; seek and you will find;
knock and the door will be opened to you."

MATTHEW 7:7 NIV

Four little gray tabby kittens sat in a row on the porch, eyes boring into the door, fur ruffling in the brisk October breeze. It was more than a stare-down. They wanted something.

Born last spring in our backyard, they were the third litter in as many years from an abandoned companion cat. We were able to hold all of them within hours of the natal event. Their mom, Tigger, trusted us so much that she allowed us to continue socializing them. Each kitten received a name to which they responded. Frisky and Mischief were two almost identical tabby males. Fluffy was a beautiful, long-haired gray princess. And then there was Rascal. The gray female tabby with huge green eyes and a white-tipped tail was just that. . .a rascal. She was the most spirited and adventuresome of the bunch, seemingly willing to try anything at least once.

As part of our socialization routine, we would take one of the kittens inside for a while so they could get used to being held and hearing "house" noises like the television and vacuum. After a while, any time the door opened, Rascal would bolt inside. We would then spend the next thirty minutes or so calling and searching, trying to find which piece of furniture she had taken refuge under.

This particular October morning, a cold front had moved through the area. Overcast, the wind picked up as the chance of rain became more apparent. The four kittens sat on the porch, staring at the back door. It was cold and they all wanted in. Badly. Surely those sweet faces would soften an old man's heart!

"Not today," my husband told them as he looked through the top glass of the storm door. "I don't have time to chase you all over the house." He closed the interior door and returned to his work.

Within a few minutes, he heard a strange scratching noise. Opening the interior door, he found Rascal hanging on the screened portion of the storm door. She continued to climb up the screen, believing that the clear, glassed portion would allow her entrance to the house. Stretching, her paws touched the glass and, meeting the slick surface, she slid off the door completely, landing in a furry heap. Undaunted, she tried this several more times.

I admire Rascal's tenacity. But many of us think that getting God to open the door of His heart and listen to us takes that same kind of determination.

Nothing could be further from the truth. We are privileged that our God says we may ask, and not only will He hear, He will provide the good things we need. Those good things might be salvation, provision, or comfort. Our assurance is that we do not ask in vain. Simply ask and it shall be given.

CRYING OUT LOUD

LYNETTE SOWELL

The righteous cry out, and the LORD hears them; he delivers them from all their troubles. The LORD is close to the brokenhearted and saves those who are crushed in spirit. A righteous man may have many troubles, but the LORD delivers him from them all.

PSALM 34:17–19 NIV

When Jean-Luc was a kitten, he chose our son Zach to be his boy. Wherever Zach went, Jean-Luc loved to follow. Mary might have had a little lamb, but Zach had Jean-Luc. Zach would climb in bed, and Jean-Luc would tuck himself in by Zach's side. When Zach watched TV, Jean-Luc napped at his feet.

During the school day, Jean-Luc somehow understood that Zach would eventually come home again. He'd lie on Zach's bed, waiting for his return. Eventually Zach was old enough to get his first job. Now Zach was gone not just during the day, but in the evenings, too. Late one afternoon, my husband left to take Zach to work, and I remained home working on the computer. I enjoyed the stillness of the house and the quiet after a busy day.

Then the howling began. We have five cats in our family, but a quick peek revealed the source of the crying. Jean-Luc was pacing the front room and the kitchen, howling. He went from room to room until he returned to the entryway and sat by the front door. The cries continued.

"Lukey, I'm here!" I called out to him as I headed back to my computer.

Jean-Luc kept howling.

"Lukey, it's okay. Zach will be home later." He ran down the hall to our room, hopped onto our bed, and I consoled him with a few pets.

Later that night after Zach returned home, I told him how much Jean-Luc had missed him. We'd never heard him howl like that before.

"He really missed you, son, and he thought he was all alone when you and Dad left."

Zach laughed. "Didn't he know you were there, working in the back of the house?"

"I guess not," I said. "I was working on the computer and everything was quiet and still." Occasionally Jean-Luc still cries when the house is quiet, but as soon as he hears someone's voice, he knows he's not alone.

Sometimes we think we're all alone, too, when really we're not. The Lord of the universe may seem far away, but in fact He's listening for our cry. He isn't far off from any one of us, and when we cry out like Jean-Luc, a cat who thinks he's all alone in the house, our Lord is swift to answer us. He invites us to come to Him, and He gives us comfort and healing. We are never alone.

ENOUGH TO LAST
NINE LIVES:
PATIENCE

*A cat is a patient listener, even when you're
telling a story for the third time. . . .*
PAM JOHNSON-BENNETT

WAITING...

DEE ASPIN

The LORD is longsuffering, and of great mercy.

NUMBERS 14:18 KJV

Rex just peed on my bathroom rug!" I looked up from the kitchen table at Carla's flushed face. She quickly added, "He doesn't usually do this anymore." EJ, her two-year-old, laughed hysterically from his booster seat. EJ and the cat are not on talking terms after too many tail-pulls. Carla banned them from being in the same room altogether.

"I'll put Rex out," I offered, running to pick up the long gray-haired squire and tossing him gently into the garage. "Meow" he bristled, granting me a sour expression. After all, he was the first one here. Even before Carla moved in, Rex had staked claim to this house.

"He owns this home," Carla conceded. "He knows it. This is *his* house—he allows *us* to live here."

It all started the day Carla moved in. The boxes lined her garage. Every time she opened the door to get another box this cat would run by her into the house.

"I chased him around the house to get him out," Carla explained. "No matter what door I went through—the garage, the front, the back—he got in. It was always a surprise! This crazy cat raced past my feet. I couldn't figure out why or what was going on.

"If I laid on the ground tired, he bit my head, then my leg. He pooped at the entrance to the garage and staked his yellow mark everywhere. It was horrid. I tried to catch this cat the first week or two, always thinking, *Why is this horrible cat in here?*

"One day a cat lady said, 'I can tell you why he's there—that is his house. Have you called the previous owners?'

"I called them to find that he had run away. They apologized and came to get him immediately. They kept him in for two weeks. Then he came back—again and again. The fourth time they said, 'We don't know what to do. Would you like to try to keep Rex?'

"After two years of biting, peeing, and pooping on everything—Rex stopped biting."

I looked at Carla amazed.

She explained, "Everyone thought I was going to take this cat to the pound. So did I, but I knew he would be killed—he was so horrible. But I couldn't stand the thought of that."

Then Carla got Honeybun, her blonde Pekingese look-alike. The dog she loves. Rex loves her, too. They sleep together and kiss each other nose to nose. Rex keeps Honeybun happy. Rex loves Carla's stepdad, Don, too. When Don sits on the couch, Rex wraps his tail around his head.

Today Carla actually likes having Rex in the house. He's not fussy. He never bites. He sits on her lap and purrs. Carla remembers thinking, *Surely if I love him, he will change*. It just took forever.

Sometimes people in our lives can seem incorrigible—downright defensive and mean-spirited. Sometimes it takes awhile for a cat, or a person, to struggle through a difficult season in life. Just as Carla waited at her expense for Rex to come around, hopefully we will ask God for the longsuffering virtue of love to wait upon our own Rexes. And remember God still waits patiently for us.

MEOW!

CONNIE PETERS

*But if we hope for what we do not yet have,
we wait for it patiently.*

ROMANS 8:25 NIV

One cold night in Pennsylvania when my husband, our two children, and I came home from visiting Grandma and Grandpa, we heard a very distinct and pronounced *ME OW*. It was so clearly annunciated, we thought at first that one of our friends was hiding behind a tree, trying to trick us.

We looked and found no one, but out from behind some bushes pranced a beautiful long-haired gray and white cat. The children and I instantly wanted to warm the poor thing up; but my husband, the sensible one, pointed out that we couldn't possibly take in all of the strays in the neighborhood.

So with determination I didn't invite the cat in, nor did I feed it, but that cat knew what he wanted. After a few days of persistent *ME OW*s, it was my husband who dubbed him Fred, allowing him to become part of our family.

Not only did Fred pick out our home and insist on getting it, Fred demanded his own way many times over. When it came to who ate first, our huge half-Saint Bernard or Fred, Fred and his *ME OW*s somehow won.

With a *ME OW*, he'd hop up on the couch and nap with me. My own Teddy Kitten. Or was I his Teddy Human?

Fred had one unusual desire for a cat. He liked water. He didn't actually swim, but he liked to sit on my son's knees when he took a bath and Fred didn't mind getting wet. He liked to watch the water go down the drain, as if he were saying farewell.

One time Fred got in trouble for following his nose. When the cat sniffed at muscle rub, my kind (I use the term loosely) husband gave in to Fred's *ME OW*s and let him have what he wanted. Poor kitty nearly rubbed his nose raw trying to get the ointment off.

Like cats, humans like to get what we want and can be as insistent as Fred with his *ME OW*s. Except, we say *ME NOW*. Sometimes we want things that are good for us, some bad, some just plain fun or quirky. The Bible tells us how to get what we want. We're to delight in the Lord. We're to train our "wanters" to want God and the things of God. And we're to be patient, waiting for God's answers, in His timing, with a godly (not a *ME NOW*) attitude.

+ROUBLED WA+ERS

SARA FOUST

My brethren, count it all joy when ye fall into divers temptations;
knowing this, that the trying of your faith worketh patience.
But let patience have her perfect work, that ye may be
perfect and entire, wanting nothing.

JAMES 1:2–4 KJV

Winchester was a feisty, black puffball of a kitten that my husband and I adopted, along with his sister kitty, soon after we were married, bringing our pet grand total to six cats and two large dogs. Our modest home had very little spare space unoccupied by boxes, dog beds, and a hodgepodge of mismatched furniture.

There was no place to put the kittens' litter box, so I decided that the spare bathroom's bathtub would be a suitable place. It was out of the way, easy to clean, and would keep the spilled cat litter confined. It was the perfect solution.

Winchester soon became very adept at chasing his sister, Annie, through the living room, into the spare bathroom, and diving over the bathtub into their litter box. He would basically stand at the doorway and leap blindly into the tub.

Before long, I began to unpack and organize all of our many boxes and soon enough there was extra space for the litter box on the floor in the spare bedroom. I moved the litter box and decided that the bathtub was so dirty it needed to soak, so I filled it about half full of water and added some dish soap.

Poor Winchester did not notice that I had moved the box and, as usual, came tearing through our living room, headed for the bathtub. He dove in, as usual, but found a terrible surprise waiting for him.

I am not quite sure how he got so wet for it seemed that as soon as the tips of his toes hit the water, he changed directions midair and streaked back into the living room, looking quite confused. He plopped down in the middle of the living room floor and began to calmly clean his wet feet, tail, and belly.

He glanced at me occasionally, still looking rather confused, but never seemed angry or upset. He was not hiding in a corner from embarrassment nor was he angrily facing the situation of being completely soaked. I realized then that he was handling the surprise with as much grace and dignity as he could muster.

That day Winchester showed me that if we could handle the little surprises, however unpleasant, that life throws our way with the grace and dignity afforded by faith in God, we would be able to smile at the end of the day regardless of what we had faced. The struggles and challenges in our daily lives help us to grow in God if we turn to Him for guidance, strength, and comfort.

Rather than reacting with anger, malice, or flippancy when faced with people or situations that are difficult, we should try to react in the way that God has instructed us: with love, patience, and understanding. By living a life daily that is filled with prayerful thought *before* action and a spirit consumed by His love, we can all find the patience to face life's troubled waters with dignity and grace.

FAT CAT:
BLESSINGS

There's a mouse house
In the hall wall
With a small door
By the hall floor
Where the fat cat
Sits all day,
Sits that way
All day
Every day
Just to say
"Come out and play."

JOHN CIARDI

tHE BOND WE SHARE

ANGELA DEAL

For as we have many members in one body, but all the members do not have the same function, so we, being many, are one body in Christ, and individually members of one another. Having then gifts differing according to the grace that is given to us, let us use them.

ROMANS 12:4–6 NKJV

Frisky and Shadow are both tabby cats. With their short, brown coats covered with matching raven-black stripes, they are almost mirror images of each other. But, in spite of their similar appearances, Frisky's and Shadow's personalities are as different as night and day.

While Frisky is laid-back and affectionate, Shadow is a feisty touch-me-not. And where Shadow is stoic and quick-witted, Frisky is lazy and slow to figure things out. But, despite their differences, they have become the best of friends. It is heart-warming to watch Frisky and Shadow interact with each other, especially when Frisky wraps his arms around Shadow's neck and gently bathes her. Oftentimes, though, their friendship takes on a more humorous tone.

For example, one evening we heard a desperate cry coming from the kitchen. Running to see what the commotion was all about, my kids and I found Frisky sprawled out on the floor, frantically hitting the bottom of the fridge with his paw. He was trying to reach for a dead mouse that lay just behind the kickboard. But, as hard as he tried, Frisky just couldn't figure out how to get to that mouse. The more he swatted the kickboard, the more agitated he became.

Since we weren't really keen on him eating the dirty rodent, my daughter finally pulled Frisky away from the fridge. But then Shadow, who had been quietly watching from a distance, surprised us. Walking over to the fridge, she took hold of the end of the kickboard with her paw. Then without any effort at all, she pulled it out of the way and reached for the mouse. She picked it up with her mouth, then walked toward Frisky and dropped it on the floor.

The kids and I burst out laughing. What seemed to be an impossible task for Frisky was nothing more than simple logic to Shadow! And because of the common bond they shared—friendship—Shadow used her skill to help Frisky out in his time of weakness.

The Bible says we have all been created with different gifts and abilities and that we are to use what God has given us to bless and encourage others. But how many times do we miss out on those opportunities, choosing instead to criticize or judge our neighbor because of these differences?

Just as Frisky and Shadow share a common bond, so do we share a common bond as Christians—our faith in the Lord Jesus Christ. May we learn to rejoice in the unique imprint of God in each other's lives and use our different gifts to strengthen the body of Christ!

GO WITH THE FLOW, ELMO

JO UPTON

Live in harmony with each other. Don't be too proud to enjoy the company of ordinary people. And don't think you know it all!

ROMANS 12:16 NLT

Elmo, a sleek, black kitten from the litter of our female cat, began life at our house. Although his physical features were average, we found ourselves charmed by his relaxed and easygoing approach to life. So when it came time to place his brothers and sisters in their new homes, we decided to keep him.

Elmo enjoyed his new setup. Without the other kittens, he had all our attention. Within a few years, he had become accustomed to being spoiled and had developed quite a number of personal rituals. One of his favorites occurred each morning after breakfast. As soon as his tummy was full, Elmo strolled to the family room to nap in a child-sized chair that belonged to my youngest daughter. He would position himself in the overly padded seat and sleep joyously for hours. This cat appreciated all the little extras life had to offer.

But then we acquired a puppy. The puppy liked the chair, too, and he had no respect for Elmo's routine. We watched as Elmo sized up the situation. At first he watched the puppy with an air that said he realized the dog wasn't as bright or worthy as himself—or even another cat! But that eventually softened and he made peace with the interloper. Soon he allowed the puppy into his "world," and they became fast friends.

Several more years passed, and one of our children brought home another kitten. Since adult cats and kittens aren't always compatible, we introduced them slowly. The kitten was hesitant, but Elmo was his usual self—relaxed and almost hospitable. As soon as he decided this new creature was staying, he just moved over and let it happen.

This continued for all of Elmo's life. As pets would come and go, Elmo adjusted, accepted, and almost seemed to enjoy the process. Part of his charm was his ability to live in harmony with every living creature that entered our home. He never tried to take top position simply because he was "first." His attitude saved us the turmoil of having pets that had to be constantly monitored and separated, and probably attributed to Elmo's long and healthy life.

Elmo seemed to know instinctively what God wants us all to understand—we should live with mutual respect for one another. We all need God's saving grace, whether king or pauper, and He has placed enjoyable traits in each of us. When we refuse pride, friendships can come from anywhere, and we're often surprised by the delightful people God places in our lives.

+HE SiSterS' WAR

LYNNDA ELL

And the effect of righteousness will be peace, and the result of righteousness, quietness and trust forever.

ISAIAH 32:17 ESV

Chloé came to America about six months before her sisters. She was travel-sick when she got here, so our other cat, George, never saw her as a threat. Within a short period, they became napping partners, curling up around each other for every catnap and tolerating each other the rest of the time.

After my daughter, Julie, completed her Peace Corps assignment, she brought Chloé's sister cats, Tiger and Bailey, home. The plan was to integrate the four cats into one family, since Julie and I would share an apartment. The sisters, however, would have no part of it. For several months, we tried every combination of cat introduction possible. All efforts resulted in poufy tails and flying fur balls.

Consequently, we kept the two pairs of cats separated. Tiger and Bailey lived in Julie's master suite. George and Chloé lived

145

in my bedroom and the rest of the house. The closest they could come to fighting was to growl and push at paws under the dividing door.

Détente reigned until one winter night when the old house settled just enough to let the latch click open on the door separating the cats. Only one member of the household heard it: Bailey. Everyone else was peacefully asleep.

When Bailey investigated the sound and discovered she could leave her territory, she began exploring. I awakened to the sound of a cat jumping up on my office chair and her low growl.

For some reason, Chloé had decided to sleep on the top of my still warm computer monitor instead of coming to bed with me. I opened my eyes to see Bailey crouched in the seat of the chair—puffed out to her biggest size—and Chloé scrambling to her feet on top of the monitor. Before I could respond, Chloé made a flying leap off the monitor, out the door, and into the living room with Bailey right behind her.

I yelled for Julie as I jumped out of bed and started after them. By this time, Chloé had made it to the sunroom and was crouched in a corner under the daybed where Bailey was trying to get to her. Tiger was halfway across the living room for her chance to get Chloé when George tackled her and they rolled over in a black and orange clawing ball of fur.

Julie reached into that catfight and came out holding George. She shoved him into my arms and started after Tiger. I closed George into my bathroom while Julie captured Tiger and got her back into the master suite. Julie then ran back to the sunroom, crawled halfway under the daybed, and dragged Bailey out. Bailey was promptly returned to her proper place, then we coaxed Chloé out from under the daybed.

After Julie and I stopped shaking, we checked for injuries. We found a few minor scratches—on us as well as the cats. It took longer to de-fur the living room than it did to de-fight the cats. Eventually, détente reigned again.

Next time the quiet of your house bothers you, thank God for its peacefulness.

FAST FOOD DELIVERY— Kitty Style

CONNIE PETERS

*Therefore, since we are receiving a kingdom that cannot be shaken,
let us be thankful, and so worship God acceptably
with reverence and awe.*

HEBREWS 12:28 NIV

Nine-year-old Aimee thought she had the coolest cat in Salida, Colorado. At first she had a hard time convincing her friends.

"That cat does nothing but sit there in the field," they'd say. It was true. Tiger would sit by the gopher holes for hours.

"He's hunting gophers," Aimee would explain.

"Does he catch them?"

"Yes."

"What does he do with them?"

"He kills them and eats them."

"Ewwww."

But that isn't what Aimee thought made him cool. Tiger knew how to ring the doorbell. He delivered gophers to the doorstep like Domino's delivered pizza.

At first he just liked to crawl on the brick ledge by the door to greet the family members as they came in. Eventually he learned that rubbing the doorbell would make a noise that would bring his family running. It was like saying, "Here humans, humans, humans." And then he discovered that he could bring his family the catch for the day, ring the doorbell, and get the attention he deserved for being such a good hunter.

Aimee's mom thought the special deliveries gross, but Aimee and her younger sister Kim thought they were great. They congratulated him with such delight that he did it again and again.

Aimee's family lived in the country, and since Tiger developed nearly a daily habit of ringing the doorbell, when it rang, they figured it was him. But they made sure they answered the door in order not to snub the occasional neighbor or mailman. And about once a month in the mild seasons, Tiger would make deliveries.

But he wouldn't ring the doorbell on command. No matter how many times Aimee and Kim would put him up on the ledge to show their friends, he would simply look at them blankly, hop down, and return to his gopher holes. But after he became a regular doorbell ringer, their friends agreed that Tiger was the coolest cat in the neighborhood.

Like Tiger, God loves attention. He loves it when we shower Him with praise and the appreciation He deserves. Of course He doesn't ring the doorbell, but sometimes while viewing His majestic creation, holding a newborn baby, or singing in a worship service, we can feel His Holy Spirit urging us to respond. He loves our company and wants to interact with us. And He is worthy to be honored and praised. He is the coolest God in the neighborhood.

†HE SAD SUNDAY

MARCIA HORNOK

*[Jesus said,] "A little while, and you will not
see Me. . .you will weep and lament."*

JOHN 16:19–20 NKJV

One Sunday morning Brad and Teri awoke to find their cat not curled up on their bed. They figured Sooty had gone out the cat door earlier than usual. They got dressed for church and filled the cat dish, but still no Sooty. Their solid black cat did not seem to be in the house.

When they walked outside to get in their car, they finally spotted her. Their beloved cat lay dead in the middle of the street.

Heartbroken, Brad carried her into the house and Teri got a towel to wrap her in. Too grieved to go to church, they phoned their relatives and closest friends to tell them Sooty had been killed.

Deciding to bury her in the backyard, Teri found a cardboard box, and Brad dug a deep hole. By afternoon, their family and friends had come to console Brad and Teri. They stood in a circle around Sooty's grave and talked about her cute antics and mischievous streaks. When the little service ended, the men filled in the grave.

For the rest of the day Brad and Teri mourned over Sooty, wondering what they would do without her. Eventually the long day ended, and they went to their bedroom to try to sleep. There was Sooty on their bed, alive and well. Some other black cat had received a proper burial that day!

Jesus told His disciples their grief over losing Him would be temporary. "Therefore you now have sorrow; but I will see you again and your heart will rejoice, and your joy no one will take from you" (John 16:22 NKJV).

Someday we who belong to Christ will have full joy over seeing Him face-to-face. Not only that, but scriptures indicate we will also be with our loved ones who have died in Christ. Death is temporary, and so is the grief it causes. In her hymn, "When We All Get to Heaven," Eliza E. Hewitt wrote, "What a day of rejoicing that will be!"

Even greater than Brad and Teri's delight over seeing Sooty again, in eternity we will be overwhelmed to be with our Savior and Lord, Jesus Christ. He will turn all our sorrows into joy.

GIMPY

CONNIE PETERS

"He who has an ear, let him hear what the Spirit says to the churches.
To him who overcomes, I will give some of the hidden manna.
I will also give him a white stone with a new name written on it,
known only to him who receives it."

REVELATION 2:17 NIV

Once upon a time in Nebraska, when the weather was starting to get cold, my sister Linda and her daughter Allie kept hearing a distressed yelping come from the pony barn, but as soon as they entered, it would stop.

After a day or two, Linda's husband brought in a tiny gray kitten. Linda called the kitten Yelp because of the pitiful noise she made. They fed her with an eyedropper, but it wasn't long before the kitty was eating independently and up and running around the house. She was so little and streaked by so fast, the kids called her Mouse. The twins, Allie's friends, called her Shadow. It was Allie who first noticed the kitten's limp. Upon further inspection, they saw that one of the kitten's feet wasn't fully formed. As the kitten grew, the limp became more pronounced, and unfortunately, she got stuck with the name Gimpy.

Just like bullies pick on the weakest kid on the playground, Gimpy had her own bully to contend with. Big, gangly Lutfi (a feline named after a VeggieTales character) would chase poor, little Gimpy, sounding like a horse galloping through. But one evening while Linda washed dishes, Lutfi slid past her on the kitchen floor with bitty Gimpy in hot pursuit. After that, Gimpy and Lutfi became friends and chased each other around the house.

Since Linda already had three house cats, she began acclimating Gimpy to outdoor life, but worried how the kitten would fare with the other cats, especially with winter coming. And then friends, a young couple, fell in love with Gimpy. Though they weren't looking for a cat, the young man once had a cat who had been maimed in an accident, so his heart went out to Gimpy.

Gimpy's new mistress gave her cats names she would call her own children if her husband would only let her. Her current cat was Rupert. All of Gimpy's names up until then described how she looked or what was wrong with her, but now she had a name of a fairytale princess, Gwendolyn Athena. So Yelp Mouse Shadow Gimpy Gwendolyn Athena lived happily ever after with Prince Rupert, indoors.

We all like fairy tales where the heroine begins humbly, struggles, marries the prince, and lives happily ever after. It may sound foolish to dream about happily-ever-after for real, but in Jesus, God promises we will live with Him in heaven, a place where we'll cry or yelp no more. And He has a new name for each of us.

CAT PLAY

GAYLE LINTZ

God. . .richly supplies us with all things to enjoy.
1 TIMOTHY 6:17 NASB

I'm sure the people who develop and manufacture toys for cats do a lot of thinking, planning, and research in their production process. They probably even play with cats. Pet stores have displays full of furry, fuzzy, and wobbly things designed to excite, amuse, and tease the nation's feline population. Some are even advertised as being able to "drive cats crazy." I don't know why that's a positive cat-toy attribute, but it's what some packages say.

The first Christmas we had T-Tat, my mother-in-law gave her a stick with a wiggly string attached and a fish toy on the end. My aunt gave her a catnip-filled butterfly. Despite the best-laid hopes and dreams of the creative people in the cat toy industry, T-Tat was unimpressed. The items got some attention for about twenty minutes. After that, they lay unused and undisturbed, gathering dust in a corner on the floor.

But T-Tat does love to play and interact with her doting caregivers. And she does have things she likes to play with. To help other cat owners, here are playthings she adores:

Rolled-up Ball of Paper—Any old (or new) piece of paper, wadded up into a ball, is one of the best cat toys ever invented. T-Tat will run, chase, jump up, and pounce down. The Amazing Rolled-Up Ball of Paper can be flying through the air, rolling across the floor, hiding in my hand, or just lying quietly on the rug, and she's on it. Due to the nature of paper, the toy has to be replaced pretty frequently. Sheets of newspaper, magazine pages, used gift wrapping, junk mail, and whatever you happen to have are great raw materials for fashioning your own Rolled-Up Ball of Paper.

Worn-out Hair Band—My wife frequently wears hair bands, and they wear out fairly quickly. The kitty only plays with one of those for about five minutes. But she plays with it for five minutes each and every day, until she loses it or it just disintegrates. We keep a stash of replacement Worn-out Hair Bands on hand.

Yarn Thing—A few years ago, my aunt wanted to learn to crochet. A friend taught her the first step, which is making a chain. She crocheted a long yellow yarn chain, put a tassel on the end of it, wrapped it up in Christmas paper, and gave it to T-Tat as a toy. Genius. It enchants her. And, if we're tired, all we need do is hang it over a doorknob, and the cat entertains herself for extended periods of time.

Today, toys for people, from infants to adults, are often flashy, noisy, and need batteries or a plug. And while *we* are plugged in, we miss the wonderful things God has given us. A setting sun (or a rising one), a starry night, blooming flowers, singing birds, a rainstorm, and a rainbow, can all teach us more than technology. Simple things *are* best, aren't they?

GRACIE BY FIRE

LINDA PANCZNER

*I waited patiently for the LORD; he turned to me and heard my cry.
He lifted me out of the slimy pit, out of the mud and mire; he set
my feet on a rock and gave me a firm place to stand.*

PSALM 40:1–2 NIV

Gracie chose me. One day when I was sitting in the family room with Boo, my black cat, a young cat nonchalantly strolled by. I had left the back door slightly propped open so Boo could enter, unaware that this stray would shortly follow. I think she was born under the back porch and benefited from the food I put out for various strays. I don't know what happened to her mother, but apparently she was seeking alternate care, and decided domesticity would do. Between extreme weather conditions and her tiny size, which put her at a disadvantage with the larger, more aggressive strays, I doubt she could have endured for long on her own. Just as she needed to be nurtured, so did I.

God doesn't give us more than we can handle, which is why

Gracie showed up when she did. Gracie's arrival helped take the sting out of the recent loss of my last grandparent and the sudden demise of Boo that soon followed her arrival. Holding Gracie on my lap, listening to her purring, she gave me something positive to focus on instead of grief. In return, I gave her the assurance that life has more to offer than merely trying to survive it. Still, I couldn't fight all of her battles.

Gracie has endured multiple tests since she walked into my house and life. Probably as the runt of the litter, she already knew something about challenges. However, living in relative comfort inside a house isn't perfect either. When she was six months old, she went in for routine spaying, but the vet discovered she was pregnant. Given her diminutive size, she wouldn't have survived giving birth, so she was freed of that danger. Thus, her surgery and recovery took longer; in fact, she returned to the vet for emergency treatment. When she came home, she faced perhaps her greatest trial because it is ongoing: Tucker, the new cat who bullies Gracie daily.

Throughout her ordeals, Gracie, like her name, is gracious about her tribulations—until the almost-fire incident. My house is cool in the winter, because heating costs are high while my paycheck is not. One night, I sat wrapped in layers in a recliner chair, while Gracie lay above me on the chair-back, her back pressed to a lightbulb for the heat it provided. I smelled something burning and looked up to see smoke coming from Gracie's back. Quickly, I swatted the burning area. She had no idea I was reacting to the smoke. Gracie leapt off the chair and looked at me with such hurt indignity. Well, the hurt part should have been blamed on the burning light, not on me. Still, I understood her indignity when I started laughing. Eventually, she forgave me, but not the lightbulb.

God blesses us with many ways to tolerate the adversities of life. Sometimes, it's the reciprocal gratification from petting a cat; other times, it's the gift of humor to put something into a better perspective.

Rip on the Roof

CONNIE PETERS

In his heart a man plans his course,
but the LORD determines his steps.

PROVERBS 16:9 NIV

After my husband and I had been married five years, we bought sixteen acres in southwest Colorado and dreamed of building a nice house and having a cat named Rip, a dog named Roar, and a bull named Snort. Soon after we moved in, a man rented our land from us to graze his cattle for the winter. The bull wasn't ours to name, but he sure did snort. And with the ruckus he made, I was glad to see him go in the spring.

Not long after, we got the kind of dog I always wanted, a Saint Bernard–golden retriever mix. With her gentle nature, she definitely was not a Roar, though, and besides, she came with name already ascribed, Amber.

When my friend needed a home for a cat, I adopted her and named her Rip. During the ten-mile drive home, I learned that Rip was a perfect name for her because in her panic, she ripped the skin off my arm with her sharp claws.

Rip looked like the cats that pose for Halloween pictures by pumpkins and perch on the end of witches' brooms—green-eyed, skinny, and black. We decided she was an outdoor cat. However, Rip decided she was an indoor cat. And since we lived in a trailer at the time, she liked to crawl up on the roof and down into the house through the open vent.

I spent a lot of time putting her out of the house, while she spent a lot of time coming back in. We had no air-conditioning, so we had to choose between a hot trailer or a persistent cat.

Since she was up on the roof frequently, that's where we put her food bowls. It was not only convenient for Rip, but it kept them away from the skunks who liked to come up on the porch at night to steal her food.

When Rip was eating or headed for the vent, my husband would sing, "You and me and Rip on the roof."

Rip was a good mouser and a good mom. She had three kittens, two short-haired gray ones and a fluffy black-and-white one who looked like Figaro on *Pinocchio*. We gave them away when they were old enough and Rip ran away when we went on vacation, never to be seen again (except on Halloween when she comes out to pose for pictures).

We never did get Roar and Snort, and we eventually sold our land and moved into town. Our plans and dreams don't always turn out the way we think they should, but we can learn to enjoy (or put up with) whatever blessings we have at the moment.

WHEN THE CAT'S OUT OF THE BAG: HOPE & FORGIVENESS

If you have a cat, congratulations. You have a relationship in which you are unconditionally loved, endlessly forgiven for your mistakes, never judged, and constantly entertained. A cat can make the stresses of your day disappear just by curling up in your lap at night.

PAM JOHNSON-BENNETT

tHE PRODiGAL CAt REtURNS

DEBRA ANN ELLIOTT

You have lived on earth in luxury and self-indulgence.
You have fattened yourselves in the day of slaughter.

JAMES 5:5 NIV

Samson the cat wandered into our garage one day and decided it was his. Funny thing is, my husband is not particularly fond of cats, but Samson changed my husband's mind that fateful day.

I heard my husband calling from the garage. "Honey?" He sounded strange.

From the tone in his voice, I assumed he had run across a lizard or racoon in the garage. I meandered downstairs and toward the garage, out of which strange noises were emanating. *Dave must have cornered a raccon,* I thought. Laughing at *that* picture, I walked into the garage.

"What's so funny?" My husband gave me one of his looks. He was not a happy man, and I was making it worse.

"What's going on in here, Dave? Did you corner a raccoon?"

"No, I didn't corner a racoon! I cornered a cat! A dirty, smelly cat."

In the corner of the garage, I spotted the cat, then tried to coax it out of its safe haven. "Here, kitty, kitty." That didn't work, so I sent Dave to get a piece of hotdog.

"We're not keeping that cat! Just so you know, I'm only going along with your plan to get it out of the garage."

"Sure, whatever you say." I had other plans for the cat that lurked behind the hot water tank. Finally, about twenty minutes after intense begging, it appeared. Dirty and smelly didn't do justice to Dave's decription of what appeared. It was one scared fur ball.

When Samson emerged, Dave backed away. My husband is afraid of cats, and Samson didn't make a good first impression.

"We've got to clean him up." I looked at Dave, who was halfway across the garage.

"Are you crazy? I already told you, no cat!"

That was six months ago and Samson is still with us. Dave decided "that cat" looked like a Samson and the name stuck. In the six months we've had him, he's grown fat and lazy. Samson comes and goes. We can't keep him cooped up. He'll disappear for several days and wander in when he pleases. Dave's back to calling Samson "that cat."

" 'That cat' lives in the lap of luxury. You spoil him way too much, Ann," he tells me.

One day Samson rubbed against my leg, and I instinctively reached down to pet him. Out the door he went! Dave didn't say a word. Not even "I told you so."

"That cat" has been gone two months now. Dave keeps reassuring me that Samson will return, just like the Prodigal Son.

I prayed Dave was right, though I blamed myself. I had spoiled "that cat." I fretted over Samson, and I almost gave up hope of his ever returning.

Today, however, I was cleaning out the garage when I heard a familiar *Meow, meow*. Samson had returned! The Prodigal Cat was home.

The Lord does not want His children living in luxury and self-indulgence, growing fat and lazy. We cannot be the Prodigal Cat. It is time for us to "come home."

tRiAL BY tuckER

LINDA PANCZNER

We are afflicted in every way, but not crushed; perplexed, but not despairing; persecuted, but not forsaken; struck down, but not destroyed; always carrying about in the body the dying of Jesus, so that the life of Jesus may also be manifested in our body.

2 CORINTHIANS 4:8–10 NASB

I have a Tucker—not a condition, though he might cause one. Tucker is my cat, my first male cat; maybe that explains him. Tucker joined me when he was six months old, and I was his third owner. Should that have been a warning? When I picked him up, he was already in his crate. I looked inside at a large, gorgeous face with big green-yellow eyes and long fur of brown, black, and tan. Once home, I opened the crate and noticed not only is his head huge, so is his body. Well, he is part Maine coon; the other part might as well be dog, or some alien species.

Tucker immediately investigated my house, my other cat, Gracie, and me, and tried to establish himself as alpha animal. Poor Gracie is constantly subjected to Tucker's abuse. Unfortunately for Tucker, I have not acquiesced to his assumptions of superiority. Whenever I scold him, he waits until I turn away to attack my ankle. My neighbor Betty advised me to spray him with water when he misbehaves; however, I'd have to carry the bottle constantly and make frequent trips to the sink for refills.

So, why is Tucker reprimanded so often? One reason is his propensity for knocking anything off of surfaces. The teacups I display are tied together through the handles and secured to a heavy weight so Tucker can't push them off. Seasonal decorations are placed in containers and weighted with a hidden rock.

Even when sleeping, Tucker distinguishes himself. His favorite position is sitting up in a chair like a person with one front paw leaning on the armrest. Another preferred position is lying on his back with his legs splayed to the sides, snoring loudly. Occasionally, he honors my lap, which can be problematic if I'm working on the computer, as he rests his paw on my hand while I try to manipulate the keyboard.

There's nothing dainty or refined about "The Tuck." He doesn't walk; he struts. He growls at stray cats, chases squirrels on the rare occasions he breaks loose, snarls at the vet, marches on the piano keys, yet drools with affection as I remove the constant tangles from his fur. He races me downstairs since he has to be first, weaves back and forth in front of me as I'm walking, and lies directly behind me when I'm standing. After my week's vacation away, he let me know how annoyed he was. I'll leave out details, other than noting that I now have four kitty litter pans placed strategically.

Tucker vexes me, but perhaps that's God's plan. Challenging situations complicate my life, but Tucker preoccupies me with his charades. If I return home in a bad mood, there's Tucker, standing tall on his back legs, looking out at me, ready to lighten my load. The Lord accepts us with all our imperfections; I should be grateful for the flaws in my cat. God gave me a distraction from my worries, and its name is Tucker.

DELBERT THE DRYER SHEET

CONNIE PETERS

*Let us draw near to God with a sincere heart in full assurance of faith,
having our hearts sprinkled to cleanse us from a guilty conscience
and having our bodies washed with pure water.*

HEBREWS 10:22 NIV

Whenever my friend Barb cleaned her house, Delbert, her tabby kitten, hindered her progress: batting the broom, crawling in drawers, chasing the vacuum cleaner cord. One day when Delbert was about three months old, Barb put a load of wash in, managed to finish the kitchen despite Delbert's playfulness, transferred the load into the dryer, and started on the bathrooms. Delbert apparently grew tired of the cleaning game and left Barb alone to scrub the bathtub.

As she worked, a sound slowly entered into her consciousness: *Thump. Thump.*

There must be a shoe in the dryer, she thought.

Thump. Thump.

I don't remember washing any shoes. She decided to check.

When she opened the dryer door, it wasn't the smell of fabric softener that hit her nose. Her heart sank as she sorted through the clothes. Where there's cat poop, there must be a cat.

She found Delbert panting beneath a pair of underwear. She held him close, repenting of her oversight and then set him on the cool floor. She watched him wobble to and fro, trying to get his land legs back, and then set him outside in his basket.

A few minutes later, she checked on Delbert. He was nowhere to be seen. She imagined him wandering off, laying his little body down, and going to kitty heaven.

She set to the task of cleaning her nasty clothes dryer. Some of the stuff had baked on. She had to throw away several articles of clothing and run the remaining items through the wash again.

Hours later, she finished and looked for Delbert. When her husband came home from work in the evening, she gave up the search and made supper.

Before the couple sat down in front of the TV, Barb opened the door in the hopes Delbert had returned. A low-flying bullet whizzed by, across the back of the couch, and up the drapery. Apparently Delbert had revived.

Eventually, he recovered from his dizzy ride, for the most part. After that, Delbert acted three dryer sheets to the wind. Every so often, he'd do daffy things like chase his tail around in circles, race up and down the draperies, or smack into a piece of furniture as if it had jumped into his path.

Sometimes our lives can be like Delbert's ride in the clothes dryer—dizzying, uncomfortable, and in stinky messes of our own making. God patiently takes us out, cleans us up, and helps us heal, even though we may act a little nutty at times.

THE CAT'S PAJAMAS: SERVING

Everything that moves, serves to interest and amuse a cat. He is convinced that nature is busying herself with his diversion; he can conceive of no other purpose in the universe.

F. A. PARADIS DE MONCRIF

CHOCOLATE CHIP COOKIES AND CATS

DEBRA ANN ELLIOTT

Each of you should use whatever gift you have received to serve others,
as faithful stewards of God's grace in its various forms.

1 PETER 4:10 TNIV

I had to bake four dozen chocolate chip cookies for the church bazaar, which was two days away. I was up to my elbows in chocolate chip cookie dough when the phone rang. I glanced at the caller ID—*Mable Whitman*. She was my next-door neighbor. What did she want this time? I debated whether to let the machine pick up or answer. I knew if I didn't answer, Miss Mable would come over.

I didn't have time for her. I had a reputation to uphold. I won best cookies two times in a row at the county fair and since then, the ladies' committee counts on me to have the best chocolate chip cookies to sell.

"Hello," I answered gruffly, frustrated that Miss Mable disturbed my cookie baking.

"Annie, is that you?" Miss Mable was barely audible.

I was almost tempted to say "You've got the wrong number," but I didn't. "Yes, Miss Mable. This is Annie."

"I've fallen and broke my hip. The paramedics are here and taking me to the hospital. Hold on."

What! What did she say? She fell and broke her hip. I felt guilty about the way I'd answered the phone. "Hello, is anyone there?"

The phone went dead. Just silence. I hung up and turned off the oven. Cookies could wait. I rushed over to Miss Mable's just as the paramedics were loading her into the ambulance.

"Miss Mable, what happened?"

She looked up at me. "Annie, I tripped over Jasper and landed hard on my hip. Take care of my precious babies."

That was all she said before the ambulance sped off. *"Take care of my precious babies,"* echoed in my head. Her precious babies were ten cats. Now what? How was I supposed to bake four dozen chocolate chip cookies for the church bazaar and watch ten cats? Miss Mable is a sweet lady, a good neighbor. She reminds me of my grandmother, but *ten cats*?

So there I was, two days before the bazaar, stuck with ten cats. I tried to corral them, but they all scurried to different parts of Miss Mable's house, hissing at me.

Annie, don't give up. I had to laugh at this awkward moment. Me, standing in the middle of Miss Mable's living room, ten cats hiding in various parts of her house, and cookies over at my house, ready to go into the oven.

I phoned the members of the ladies' committee and informed them about Miss Mable. Imagine my surprise when they offered to help me bake the cookies and watch the cats, too!

It took Miss Mable Whitman and her ten cats to show me God gives us many gifts, and we are to serve others, not just ourselves. I thought my gift was to serve through baking. I was wrong! My gift is to serve others as a faithful steward in whatever form.

WHAT THE CAT DRAGGED IN

DEBRA ANN ELLIOTT

Each man will be like a shelter from the wind and a refuge from the storm, like streams of water in the desert and the shadow of a great rock in a thirsty land.

ISAIAH 32:2 NIV

"Annie, can you come here?" I heard my husband's voice floating from the kitchen. "Look what the cat dragged in!" Underneath the kitchen table sat our cat Delilah, and under her paw sat a lizard!

"Oh my! She has a lizard." I couldn't believe Delilah had brought a *lizard* into my kitchen! I know lizards are God's creatures, too, but I can't stand them—never have, never will.

"You get that lizard away from her," I commanded Dave.

"How do you suppose I do that?" Dave had a point. Delilah wasn't about to turn loose her prized possession.

"I don't know! Just get rid of *that thing*!" The lizard was squirming underneath Delilah's paw. We had to act quickly or we'd have a reptile loose in the house.

I had a plan. "I'll distract Delilah and you grab the lizard."

My husband didn't look happy. "Me?"

"You don't expect *me* to grab that thing, do you?" That's just what he was thinking. Dave doesn't like lizards either. Just when we were getting ready to distract Delilah, the interloper made its move. I jumped, Delilah pounced, and Dave ran after the lizard. Off we went on a lizard hunt! I starting laughing, maybe a little too much.

"What's so funny?" Dave didn't look amused.

"Well, let's see. We've got a crazed cat and a lizard running amok through our house."

"*Not* funny!" Dave was right, of course. Delilah we could deal with, but a scared lizard was another matter. I knew we had to trap that thing before it took up permanent residence in our house. Delilah was right on my heels. *Meow, meow.* She wanted her play toy back. Dave was trying to find something to contain the lizard. I was trying not to panic.

We cornered the lizard about twenty minutes after we started our hilarious chase. It was hiding in the bathtub. Dave gently placed the lizard in a plastic container. Delilah kept swatting at it, trying her best to get the lizard.

"Now what?" I looked at my brave husband.

"I guess we could turn it loose."

"You can't do that! Delilah would only bring it back inside."

"Any other suggestions?"

I wanted to flush it down the toilet, but I knew that was wrong. "I guess we could keep it in an aquarium for Cameron."

"Are you serious?"

"No, but what other choice do we have? If we let it go, Delilah will bring it right back in." I held the lizard in its plastic container while Dave went into the garage to find the aquarium. I was thankful it couldn't get out.

It is one of God's creatures, I kept telling myself. Were we to give this lizard shelter from the wind and refuge from the storm?

Two years have passed. Our household now consists of three very unhappy cats and one very happy lizard!

OUR BEST DOG WAS A CAT

NICK FULLER (AS TOLD TO MARCIA HORNOK)

Now he who plants and he who waters are one...
for we are God's fellow workers.

1 CORINTHIANS 3:8–9 NKJV

I don't know how our cat learned his behavior patterns, but it seemed to us that, except for purring, he acted like a dog. Every morning this pure black, long-haired tom would wait for me at the foot of the stairs. "Good morning, Mr. Purrrl," I would say.

Meow, he would reply.

Purrl loved to fetch, and although he never learned to retrieve the paper, he did enjoy reading it with me. As soon as I sat in my recliner and opened the first section, he would leap into my lap and purr until I finished the news.

When I came into the house after work every day, Purrl would greet me with his affectionate *Meow—much nicer than loud yipping or barking*, I thought.

When my wife and I worked in the yard, our cat stayed near us, batting at butterflies or chasing his tail. He would even walk behind us when we took a stroll.

Mr. Purrl is gone now, but my wife and I still say, "The best dog we ever had was a cat."

Cats are not known for their loyalty, but Purrl seemed devoted to us and appreciative of our attentions. Perhaps he somehow surpassed his self-serving instincts in order to focus on us.

I should be this way with God. Greet Him every morning. Sit on His lap, as it were, and enjoy His presence as I read His Word. Follow Him in my walk of faith. Look for Him to "show up" every day in my circumstances, interruptions, answers to prayer, and interactions with people.

And when I work in God's kingdom-garden, preparing soil, planting seeds, and nurturing young seedlings, I need to remember that He is not only with me, but I am yoked together with Him. Some Bible verses even call us His "fellow workers" (1 Corinthians 3:9; 2 Corinthians 6:1).

Mr. Purrl's devotion to us, his caregivers, can remind me to be loyal to the One who takes care of me and empowers me to serve Him. I must deny my self-preoccupation and focus on what He wants. Pleasing Him should be my daily desire, duty, and delight.

tHE KitTY ORPHAN tRAiN

CONNIE PETERS

Religion that God our Father accepts as pure and faultless is this:
to look after orphans and widows in their distress and to keep oneself
from being polluted by the world.

JAMES 1:27 NIV

When my sister and I (ages eight and five) found a stray kitten, we were determined to find it a home. Dad would not let us keep cats because they killed bunnies. Dad, being a hunter, liked the rabbit population kept up. Most of the neighbors preferred dogs for this reason.

We lived in the country, so a trek around the neighborhood involved a considerable distance. When we'd knock on the door, usually a lady would answer, smile down at us and the pathetic kitty, and politely say, "No, thank you." I enjoyed meeting neighbors we had never met before.

In my five-year-old mind, we were doing the right thing. We didn't notice it was getting dark. Mom and Dad did. And when the station wagon pulled up beside us, our parents weren't happy.

I stood in the living room, wondering why they had yelled at my sister and not me. We were guilty of doing the same thing—aiding and abetting cats. (Or maybe something to do with staying out after dark and going to strangers' houses.) Even though I didn't understand why they were holding my older sister responsible, I appreciated someone else taking the brunt of their ire.

About thirty years later, my husband, two children, and I moved from Colorado to Pennsylvania, and settled in my old neighborhood. The area had transformed from "no cats allowed" to "cats welcome," and we seemed to be living along the kitty orphan train. Stray cats often followed us home.

Our first response was to ignore them, hoping they'd continue down the road. If they hung around, we tried to find homes for them. I liked one ginger-colored kitten so much I was beginning to give in to the temptation to keep her. But when a neighbor asked if she could have her, I handed the kitten over, hoping my kids wouldn't be heartbroken.

I needn't have worried, not about that anyway. As I was saying good-bye to Ginger out the front door, my children came in the back with Frisky. The tabby cat eventually became the mother of Geordi and Data. My dad, old and having forgotten his prejudice against cats, loved watching the two kittens play.

God has a soft spot in His heart for orphans. In the Bible, James says God considers our religion pure and faultless when we are kind to orphans and widows and when we keep ourselves from worldliness. God had pity on us, spiritual orphans, and sent Jesus to take our punishment so we could be adopted into His family.

When I asked my sister about the childhood incident, she didn't even remember it. The one who receives pardon is more affected than one who receives punishment.

CAt WitH A CAuSe

JO UPTON

Therefore, my dear brothers, stand firm. Let nothing move you.
Always give yourselves fully to the work of the Lord,
because you know that your labor in the Lord is not in vain.

1 CORINTHIANS 15:58 NIV

I remember clearly the ruckus outside our kitchen door that spring morning many years ago. The unknown commotion caused the entire family—all five of us—to jam into the small doorway in hopes of catching a glimpse of the reason behind the unexpected disturbance. At first, all we could see was our very large dog, a German shepherd, standing over his feeding dish. He was snarling and growling with such intensity, we felt sure he must have cornered someone trying to enter our home, or at least a deadly snake, and had pinned it to the ground.

Imagine our surprise when we saw, instead of a worthy adversary, a very small black-and-white kitten. We watched as the tiny intruder stood his ground against a very confused dog. Seems the kitten was hungry, and he wasn't about to let the larger

183

owner of the food dish stop him from getting what he wanted. We watched in amazement as this miniscule ball of fur hissed and postured, totally disregarding the fact that he was out of his league. His body language said, "I'm here. . . .I'm eating. . . .and you can't stop me."

My father called the dog off, but as far as the kitten was concerned, it was simply a nice gesture. He had already laid claim to the contents of that dish, and with or without our help, he was going to enjoy the fruits of his labor. My dad was impressed by this very determined kitten. His tenacity won him not only that meal, but also the distinction of being our first family cat. His moment of standing firm had brought unexpected dividends.

Sometimes in our spiritual life, we identify more with the kitten than we like to admit. Circumstances and situations beyond our control loom over us, bringing fear and uncertainty, and the nagging thought that we're in over our heads. Our first impulse may be to run and hide. . .or simply give up the fight. But it's at that exact moment we need to try the kitten's approach—dig in and decide to stay the course. From our vantage point, the outcome of perseverance is hard to calculate—will our efforts really make a difference? Scripture says we already have our heavenly Father's promise that nothing is done in vain. That's a pretty solid reason to keep on trying!

THE CAT WHO SWALLOWED THE CANARY: OBEDIENCE

*The cat lives alone, has no need of society,
obeys only when she pleases, pretends to sleep
that she may see more clearly, and scratches
everything on which she can lay her paw.*

FRANÇOIS R. CHATEAUBRIAND

tHE CAt WHO UNDERStOOD ENGLISH

MARCIA HORNOK

This is love for God: to obey his commands.
And his commands are not burdensome.

1 JOHN 5:3 NIV

When Ann was nineteen, she acquired a gray and peach kitten and named her Daisy. The cuteness of this soft, blue-eyed kitten masked her wild nature. Although Daisy resisted being tamed, Ann kept her for a year, then moved to a different apartment with a roommate.

Daisy did not appreciate the new arrangement. She tore up curtains, clawed furniture, and raced through rooms at full speed. Not wanting to get rid of Daisy, Ann asked her mother, Ellen, to keep her.

"I know that cat's wild nature. I don't think it will work," Ellen said, "but I can at least give it a trial run."

When Daisy came to live with Ellen, Ellen decided to have a frank talk with the cat. She held Daisy up to her face and warned her, "You will live here as long as you behave. You will not tear up the drapes; you will not scratch furniture; you will not destroy anything in the house. Nothing like that will happen here. In return, I will take good care of you." The whole time Ellen talked, Daisy's blue eyes stared at her as if she comprehended.

Amazingly, she became a well-behaved house cat. Although Daisy remained aloof and unpredictable, Ellen had no problems with her, except for one incident a few years later.

Ellen was hosting a Bible study, and the ladies were sitting around her oval dining room table. One of the women tended to monopolize the conversation and loved to talk about herself. On this day she was telling the other ladies about everything she was allergic to. She ended by saying, "And I'm allergic to cats."

At that exact moment, Daisy came out of nowhere, leaped onto the table directly in front of the complaining woman, and stared in her face defiantly. The startled woman gasped. Ellen immediately brushed Daisy off the table, scolding her, while the other ladies tried to suppress laughter. To Ellen's knowledge, the cat had never jumped on the table before and never did it again.

Now, Daisy probably did not understand English, and her behaviors were coincidental, but what about us? We have God's instructions in our own language. He tells us how to behave and what not to do if we want to please Him. His requirements for His children are not hard to understand but can be difficult to carry out because they go against our "wild" nature. However, like Daisy no doubt discovered, it is much more pleasant to live in harmony with the Owner's guidelines than to follow our instincts and suffer the consequences.

tHE FACE OF tEMPtAtion

CHUCK MILLER

*"I have fellowship offerings at home; today I fulfilled my vows.
So I came out to meet you; I looked for you and have found you! . . .
I have perfumed my bed with myrrh, aloes and cinnamon.
Come, let's drink deep of love till morning."*

PROVERBS 7:14–15, 17–18 NIV

Pookie loved anything soft. Anything soft and furry was even better. Anything soft, furry, and warm was a temptation beyond Pookie's power to resist. Pookie was Dave's little calico. Dave was house-sitting for a friend, and had to take Pookie along. Dave's friend had dogs, but Pookie had dealt with dogs before, or thought she had.

Pookie was investigating this different house, when she came across an extraordinary temptation. Standing in the living room, she could see two mountains of soft, furry warmth on the hardwood floor in the dining room. "Mountains" is what the homeowner's two 150-pound Great Pyrenees, curled up and sleeping with their backs to the door, must have looked like to a little calico. She had to investigate. This looked like heaven on earth.

Out of nowhere, one mountain of fur raised a huge head and looked at her. Pookie turned and sprinted for all she was worth—except that the floor might as well have been ice. She spun her wheels, her little legs a blur for three or four seconds, just like in the cartoons, until she finally got some traction, hit the living-room carpet, and shot up the stairway and under the bed that her papa's suitcase was on.

She thought she was safe, until the family's dachshund got curious about this new little beast in his house and crawled under with her. Poor Pookie shot from under the bed to another bedroom, where she hid under another bed, and Dave mercifully closed the door to save her from any more doggie surprises.

Temptations. Big or little, they look so good. They can come clear out of the blue—soft, furry, warm, comfortable. They can be what you've waited for, for so long. So good. And so dangerous. Pookie thought she had finally arrived. The mountains of warm fur were what she'd been born for, or so she thought. Temptations can seem so right, made to order for us, when they're really so wrong. James said it: "But each one is tempted when, by his own evil desire, he is dragged away and enticed. Then, after desire has conceived, it gives birth to sin; and sin, when it is full-grown, gives birth to death" (James 1:14–15 NIV).

Pookie was lucky: She was enticed, but saw the "full-grown" face of her temptation before she got too close. These warnings from scripture can be, for us, the face of that Great Pyrenees rising, showing us the danger. Something that's too good to be true, or too good to be good, carries its own danger. Be discerning, especially regarding things that feel particularly pleasant; and be careful, ready to do what it takes to get away!

Pookie's story has a happy ending. She and the dachshund became friends. And she decided to do her snuggling with her papa. Good choice. No temptations there.

RHOADY tHE GRANDCAt

MARCIA HORNOK

*Those who live according to the sinful nature
have their minds set on what that nature desires.*

ROMANS 8:5 NIV

Even as a kitten, Rhoady resisted being tamed. Wild and free-spirited, the tabby never purred. She responded to human touch with an arched back, raised tail, and hissing. For some reason, this pleased her owner, Ron. Rhoady lived in Ron's apartment for a year. When Ron moved to a college dorm, he begged his parents, Andy and Doris, to take care of Rhoady.

"That mean thing? She'll bite the hand that feeds her," Andy said.

"Please," Ron begged. "It's only for a few years. After all, she's your grandcat, and I don't want to ask anyone else."

"What you mean is no one else will have her," Andy said, but he agreed to try it.

When Ron brought the cat to his parents' home, he handed them a leash and cat harness and said, "Rhoady is a house cat. I'm afraid if she gets out the door, she'll run away, so whenever you take her outside, be sure to put this harness on her."

After Ron bid his dear Rhoady farewell, Andy and Doris looked at each other with the same question on their minds: *Which of us wants to risk our life getting Rhoady harnessed up?*

They decided they would never let the cat outside. However, one day someone opened the back door and Rhoady shot out before they could stop her. They called and called, but she seemed intent on exploring the pasture. When Andy tried to catch her, Rhoady ran farther away. Hours passed. Andy and Doris worried about how to tell their son his cat had disappeared.

That evening Rhoady meowed at the door. Evidently "Rhoady the house cat" loved being outside. It tamed her somehow. She soon became an agreeable pet. She started twining around Andy's legs in the mornings as her master ate breakfast. Andy would leave a little milk and cereal in the bottom of the bowl and push it aside. This signaled Rhoady to jump up on the counter and enjoy the treat. Andy admits he spoiled Rhoady but "that's what grandparents do," he told his son.

When Ron finished college and took his cat back, he promised he would not keep Rhoady confined inside. The cat's nature had changed from wild to mild once she had the freedom of the outdoors.

So it is with us. Before we become Christians, it is our nature to resist God and go astray. When confronted with Christ, we arch our backs and hiss at the simplicity of what God offers. However, once we give up our own way and submit our wild and sinful nature to the authority of Christ, we learn to enjoy our new Master and return His love.

When Rhoady was set free, her nature changed. Likewise, God gives us a new nature when He sets us "free from the law of sin and death" (Romans 8:2).

tHE GUILtY-CAt WALk

MARCIA HORNOK

*For whoever shall keep the whole law,
and yet stumble in one point, he is guilty of all.*

JAMES 2:10 NKJV

After two years, Charlie had his calico cat so well trained that she never disobeyed. Sweet-tempered Cady seemed content to live indoors but also enjoyed the yard, which was completely enclosed by a five-foot fence.

One day Cady played outside while Charlie worked on the landscaping. Suddenly she jumped the fence and disappeared.

It shocked Charlie, because Cady had never done anything like that before. He hurried out the gate to pursue her, but what he saw gave him another surprise. Cady had gone about fifty yards down the street, walking sideways like a crab. She maneuvered her legs in that unnatural way so she could keep looking back toward the house.

Although amused by how awkward Cady looked, Charlie had to be stern with her. "You get back here right now."

Cady scampered back immediately. She never jumped the fence or left the yard again.

I don't know if cats feel guilt, but Cady certainly knew she was doing something against the rules. That happens with us Christians, too.

At times I defy God's boundaries and jump the fence. Even if no one else on earth knows what I have done, sin is never secret. God knows and I know. A guilty conscience will disrupt my spiritual walk and make me feel awkward.

I know I need to confess my sin and turn around (repent), but sometimes I want to keep enjoying the pleasures of self-will. The problem with that is the longer I let it go, the farther away I get from fellowship with God.

Despite our willfulness and wrong choices, and even when we ignore our guilty conscience, God faithfully calls us back.

Cady obeyed her master's call, and so should we.

A Contrite Kitty

Ardythe Kolb

*The sacrifices of God are a broken spirit, a broken and
a contrite heart—these, O God, You will not despise.*

Psalm 51:17 NKJV

Snickle, Grandma's gray tiger-striped cat, knew how to get anything he wanted from her. His attitude probably gave all cats a bad reputation—he was temperamental, spoiled, and merely tolerated people. He controlled his universe.

He was also picky about meals. He preferred raw beef liver and turned up his nose at canned food. Grandma complied with his finicky appetite and always cut the liver into bite-sized pieces.

Grandma filled letters with his antics. "Guess what Snickle learned to do this week. He jumps up on the table and scampers around under the tablecloth. It's so cute! I can't stand to punish him." He destroyed a centerpiece the first time he tried it, but Grandma didn't stop him. She just left the table bare except for the cloth.

One day she hosted a bridal shower for the daughter of a friend from church. Since Snickle was notorious for presenting guests with trophies he'd captured outside, Grandma closed him in a bedroom with a bowl of milk and some liver.

But someone opened the door.

The shower was moving along nicely. After the bride exclaimed in delight over her gifts, the guests visited, while carefully balancing plates and cups of punch. Grandma had flowers and wedding decorations arranged as the focal point around the food and dishes. Everything was lovely and no one noticed a little lump that appeared under the tablecloth among the decor.

A particularly genteel lady sat near the table, taking dainty bites of cake, when the tablecloth suddenly erupted. Dishes, flowers, and food toppled as Snickle flew from his hiding place, landing in the lap of Ms. Proper. Punch splattered, and her plate landed on the carpet. Snickle dropped a partially chewed chunk of liver in her lap, jumped to the floor, and proceeded to devour the fallen cake.

The poor lady sputtered, "Dear Jesus! What on earth happened?" Grandma was mortified. Everyone jumped to the rescue, but who could hold back laughter as they took in the chaotic scene? First a chuckle or two could be heard, and before long the room was filled with women roaring at the hilarity of the situation. Even the lady with liver in her lap laughed till tears ran down her powdered cheeks. After the cleanup, when guests prepared to leave, they all agreed, "Edith, we'll never forget this shower!"

Afterward Grandma began to demand better behavior from Snickle. Retraining took patience, but eventually he realized that obedience has some great rewards.

Most of us struggle with the notion that we're not the only one who matters. After we've made some big blunders, God works with us to give us a contrite heart. Life is more beautiful when we realize we're not the center of the universe, even though we may feel like our hearts are breaking during the process.

WHAt tHE KîttY WANtS

GAYLE LINTZ

"For I know the plans I have for you," declares the LORD, *"plans to prosper you and not to harm you, plans to give you hope and a future."*

JEREMIAH 29:11 NIV

T-Tat scampered between my legs, racing from the kitchen into the living room. What could have excited her so? She'd been clonking around in the kitchen just a few minutes earlier, and I'd thought she'd been pushing her food dish across the floor. She ran past me now and jumped onto her favorite windowsill where she often spent hours, tracking the birds and squirrels in the backyard below. I walked over to investigate and saw, *oh, my!* Apparently, she'd been chasing a small mouse, whose furry rump and wiggly tail now dangled from her mouth.

"Give me that," I said. I gently held T-Tat's head and tugged at the little rodent until the cat let go. *Yuck.* I quickly took the gray mouse, sealed it in a plastic bag, and dropped it in the trash. T-Tat padded behind and looked at me quizzically.

"Good kitty." I gave her a treat and went to explain to my

wife how our alert feline had caught a very unwanted pest. I rubbed T-Tat between her ears and under her chin. "You are a very, very good kitty."

I looked carefully around the kitchen, trying to locate the mouse's entry point. I knew the upstairs neighbors had seen mice, also. I guess they're inevitable in an old Brooklyn brownstone; still, I didn't see any holes or spaces and thought our pest problem was short-lived.

Two days later, T-Tat bolted by me again, another mouse carcass held between her teeth. She jumped onto the windowsill and stared at me.

"Oh, you good kitty." I reached to take this mouse. Nothing doing. T-Tat turned away from me and held her prey tightly.

"Come on. Give me the mouse. Please." No way.

I imagined her attitude. "No, sir. I had a nice fun toy like this before, and you took it away, and you never gave it back. I'm keeping this one."

After a short struggle, I overpowered her, got the mouse, and disposed of it. Two treats and much scratching and praise later, T-Tat was still aloof. How disappointed she must have been. She had found something interesting and anticipated a lively afternoon of playing and pouncing and chasing. She might even have invited me into her play. But I had spoiled it all.

Much to her frustration, I had an entirely different viewpoint. But I am the one in charge here, and I do know best. Really. Mouse in the house? No, T-Tat. No.

I'm glad that the Master of my house, the One whom we serve, is always on alert. When an activity looks thrilling to us or some interesting choice presents itself, He knows what's best and helps us make good decisions. I'm sure He doesn't want vermin in His house, either.

PURR-SEVERANCE!

BETTY OST-EVERLEY

Blessed is the man who perseveres under trial, because when he has stood the test, he will receive the crown of life that God has promised to those who love him.

JAMES 1:12 NIV

Many years ago, my husband, Terry, had two male orange tabby cats. The older one was named Socnees, the previous owner bestowing this unusual moniker because of some obscure Greek fable he recalled. Terry never bothered to change his name. When a female cat down the street had a litter, it was obvious that Socnees was the father. Feeling a little embarrassed or perhaps guilty that his cat was responsible, Terry offered to take one of the kittens. The tomcat, nearly identical in coloring and markings to his father, became known as Socnees, Jr., or JR for short.

A large cat, JR had personality plus. Super-friendly, he would rub against the legs of guests and hop onto unsuspecting laps, purring easily. He was laid back and nothing seemed to ruffle or upset him. And he loved to sunbathe outdoors. JR had a penchant for stretching out on top of Terry's car as it stood in the circular driveway. He would lie there contentedly for hours on end.

It turned out that JR didn't really care which cars he stretched out on. It didn't have to be Terry's; anyone's would do. So when Terry had people over, they were sometimes surprised when it came time for them to leave. The scene was played out over and over.

"Your cat won't get off my car."

"Oh, sure he will."

"Well, I tried shooing him off and that didn't work. He's right in the middle of the roof, so of course, I can't reach far enough to move him. He doesn't respond to poking. He just looks at me with those big eyes, yawns, and goes back to sleep. I even started the engine. Still won't budge."

"Go ahead. Back out of the driveway."

Looking questioningly at their host, the guests would oblige by carefully moving their car out into the street. JR would still be on the roof, seemingly oblivious to what was happening. People would even honk, stop, and point to the feline on the roof of the car. It was quite a spectacle! Only when the car started moving faster than twenty-five miles per hour did JR finally figure the person was dead serious about leaving, and he'd jump off, returning to the house to find yet another car on which to sunbathe.

Perseverance means to continue to (or try to) do something despite difficulties. To be steadfast, to hang on and be tenacious, maintaining the course in spite of discouragement. JR obviously had perseverance down to a science.

How are you in the perseverance department? When the

answer to a few prayers doesn't come quickly, or when there are no easy solutions to questions or situations, what do you do? Do you want to give up?

Perseverance is oftentimes a test of our character, a test for which we will be blessed when the testing is over. So, hang in there! *Purr*-severe!

†HE Ki††Y-CA† PARADE

CONNIE PETERS

"I tell you the truth, you are looking for me, not because you saw miraculous signs but because you ate the loaves and had your fill." ... *Then they asked him, "What must we do to do the works God requires?" Jesus answered, "The work of God is this: to believe in the one he has sent."*

JOHN 6:26, 28–29 NIV

I don't travel fourteen hours to eastern Nebraska in order to sightsee. (After you've seen one cornfield, you've seen them all.) I go there to visit my sister Linda and her family. But I do see one of my favorite sights, the Kitty-Cat Parade. My sister's family keeps twenty-some cats on their farm, and when it's feeding time, felines come running from every direction. It's quite a sight.

Besides always having a lot of cats around, between friends of Linda's daughters and kids she babysits, she always seems to have extra children around. Her kitchen reminds me of the show

ER where there's continual action and interaction. A scene from Linda's kitchen may be of her standing at the counter, chopping vegetables for a salad. There's a constant back-and-forth exchange between Linda and the kids, along with the rhythmic *squeak* and *bang* of the screen door.

"Mom, where are the markers?"

"In that drawer." *Squeak! Bang!*

"Mom, Laurie's playing in the mud."

"Take her to the swings." *Squeak! Bang!*

"Mom, the cats are getting in the van."

"Get them out and close the van door." *Squeak! Bang!*

Once, one of her charges busied himself collecting rocks. After a few minutes, he had too many to hold, so *(Squeak! Bang!)* he asked my sister for a bucket. She gave him one from a stack on the back porch. After a bit of rock hunting, the little boy came back in *(Squeak! Bang!)* and said, "Your cats are sure friendly!" He got a drink of water and went out again. *(Squeak! Bang!)*

After thinking about that a second, she put down her paring knife and went out to see about the friendly kitties *(Squeak! Bang!)*, and sure enough all the cats had gathered. She had given him an identical bucket to the one her family uses to feed the cats. He was like the Pied Piper leading the children from Hamelin. As he collected rocks, the entire Kitty-Cat Parade followed him around the farm.

In Bible times, when the crowds followed Jesus around, most of the time it wasn't due to loyalty, but to get something to eat, to be healed, or to be forgiven. Today, people follow God for the same reasons. Let's not be like the Kitty-Cat Parade, following the Master only because of what's in His bucket. Instead, let's pursue the Father who carries the bucket. And Jesus is the door to the Father. *Squeak! Bang!*

CONTRIBUTING AUTHORS

Anna M. Aquino has been passionately serving the Lord for over twenty years. Anna was most recently published in *My Dad My Hero*. She is the author of eight yet-to-be published books, four screenplays, two children's book series, and two devotionals. To learn more about Anna, visit www.annamaquino.com and www.annamaquino.blogspot.com.

Dee Aspin, author, speaker, and life coach, has spent twenty-five years in Christian ministry, currently through the Juvenile Justice Chaplaincy. She loves romping with her happy dogs, a yellow lab, Sammy, and her miniature schnauzer, Benji. A guest writer for CBN.com, she just published her first book, *Lord of the Ringless*.

Angela Deal resides in Alberta, Canada. She and her husband, Dwain, have six children between the ages of thirteen and twenty-one. Angela works part-time as a self-employed janitor and also homeschools her three youngest children. When she has time to spare, she enjoys reading and writing.

Author **Katherine Douglas** has enjoyed the company of cats since she was a toddler. She and her husband, Mark, have recently made the switch from city life to country living. They're looking to make friends with the "squatter cats" who have made themselves at home in their barn.

Lynnda Ell has been an active Christian for more than fifty years. She is a mother of three and a grandmother of five. She and her ninety-year-old mother share a home in New Orleans. She survived polio, a marriage meltdown, and Hurricane Katrina. Lynnda blogs at www.passionateforthegloryofgod.blogspot.com.

Debra Ann Elliott has a driving passion for writing. She has been writing since the age of fifteen. Her first collection of poetry was published in June 2008. Debra also writes an online Christian column about the effects of abortion. She currently resides in Alabama with her husband, daughter, and grandson.

Sara Foust began writing when she was four years old, with her first story being a simplified version of *The Gingerbread Man*. She is now a home-based medical transcriptionist. The mother of two beautiful daughters, she still enjoys writing (when she can find the time). Her family lives in Clinton, Tennessee.

Darlene Franklin is the author of four novels and two novellas with Barbour Publishing, and contributor to several devotional books, including *365 Daily Whispers of Wisdom* and *The Book Lover's Devotional*. A full-time writer, she makes her home in Oklahoma City and enjoys being near four generations of family.

Katherine A. Fuller grew up in New England, a tomboy/bookworm. In good weather, she climbed trees. In bad, her nose was in a book. Writing seemed a logical progression to her passion for reading. Katherine now resides on an organic farm in Maryland with her husband, mother, and a family of friends.

Glenn A. Hascall is an accomplished writer with credits in more than fifty books. He has written articles that have appeared in such places as the *Wall Street Journal*. He's also an award-winning broadcaster, lending his voice to national radio and television networks.

Marcia Hornok has been freelance writing and editing for twenty-five years. Her work has appeared in over sixty publications, and includes six curriculum books. In 2001, she became the managing editor of *CHERA Fellowship*. Her husband is a pastor in Salt Lake City, where they have raised their six children.

Ardythe Kolb and her husband owned and operated a successful Christian bookstore for thirteen years. She now works as a full-time freelance writer and is on the board of Heart of America Christian Writers' Network. She loves travel, reading, target practice, and spending time with her children and grandchildren.

Meredith LeBlanc retired from being a teacher and librarian in 2006, and then began writing in earnest. She has written several children's books and has an historical romance in progress. After living in four states, Kingston Springs, Tennessee, has become her home. Meredith is a member of the Middle Tennessee Christian Writers group.

Gayle Lintz has written preschool teaching materials (Sunday school, discipleship, Vacation Bible School) for Lifeway Christian Resources for several years. He has also been published in various Christian devotional periodicals. Gayle is a member of Calvary Baptist Church in Waco, Texas.

Chuck Miller lives in Toledo, Ohio. He taught at Toledo Christian High School, has been a hospital chaplain, and currently works as a surgical tech and freelance writer. He has been published in *Dogma* by Katherine Douglas, in *Northcoast* magazine, and in the *Ancient Paths* annual literary anthology, edited by Skylar Burris.

Betty Ost-Everley is an animal lover. From the first time she laid eyes on a cuddly kitten, she was hooked. A parent to three indoor cats, when Betty's not working as an administrative assistant, she divides her time between family, church, her neighborhood, and writing. She's also an advocate for feral cats.

Linda Panczner loves writing; just recently the nagging voices in her head said "go public." That and the fact her teaching job was cut in half indicated it was time to pursue other options. God closes one door and points to another, but we still have to push it open.

Connie Peters has been writing children's and adult fiction, devotions, and poetry for over twenty-five years. Her work has appeared in many publications including *Wounded by Words* by New Hope Press, *Cup of Comfort* anthologies, *Focus on the Family*, and many Sunday school take-home papers, magazines, and newsletters.

Rachel Quillin lives with her husband, Eric, and their six children on a dairy farm in Ohio. Her main focus is to serve the Lord in any way possible. She is active in her church, enjoys homeschooling her kids, doing freelance writing when possible, and is never bored!

Janet Rockey is a member of FWA, ACFW, and Word Weavers. She has studied under authors Gayle Roper, Jeanette Windle, and Mark Mynheir at Florida Christian Writers Conferences. Janet lives with her husband, Tom, and their two cats in Tampa, Florida. Visit her blog at: www.rockeywrites.blogspot.com.

Lynette Sowell is an award-winning author of eight fiction titles for Barbour Publishing. When she's not working her day job, Lynette squeezes in writing at night and on the weekends. She enjoys teaching adult Sunday school at her church, escaping to Austin with her husband, and is always in search of the perfect road trip. Lynette is a Massachusetts Yankee by birth and Texan by choice, where she lives with her husband, two teenagers, and five cats that have their humans well-trained.

Christena Struben has been a born-again Christian since 1973. As a retired educator, her goal is to use her time to create stories that will draw others to Christ. Christena has written curriculum and has just completed her first novel, *Faith Forward*. She holds an MLA from Johns Hopkins University.

Jo Upton lives in Georgia. She is married with four children and four grandchildren. She began her writing career more than twenty years ago, specializing in Christian and family-related articles and books. Through the years, she has loved—and been loved by—a number of special feline friends.

David Wandering lived in the Philippines for nine years, where he began his family, started a center for street children, and took in a stray cat named Arwen. Much of his writing comes from his experiences of the vibrant life he had in the Philippines. David now lives with his wife and three daughters in central Pennsylvania. Sadly, Arwen had to stay behind in the Philippines.

Cheryl Elaine Williams is a freelance writer residing in Pittsburgh, Pennsylvania. Cheryl is retired from the postal service and keeps busy with church activities, gardening, and volunteer activities. She has published children's and teen's short stories in the Christian marketplace and has contributed to the *Chicken Soup* series.

SCRIPTURE INDEX

OLD TESTAMENT

New Testament

Other Heavenly Humor titles from Barbour Publishing

Heavenly Humor for the Dog Lover's Soul
978-1-60260-859-7

Heavenly Humor for the Woman's Soul
978-1-60260-030-0

Heavenly Humor for the
Chocolate Lover's Soul
978-1-61626-245-7

Heavenly Humor for the Mother's Soul
978-1-61626-254-9